FIORDLAND UNDERWATER
New Zealand's Hidden Wilderness

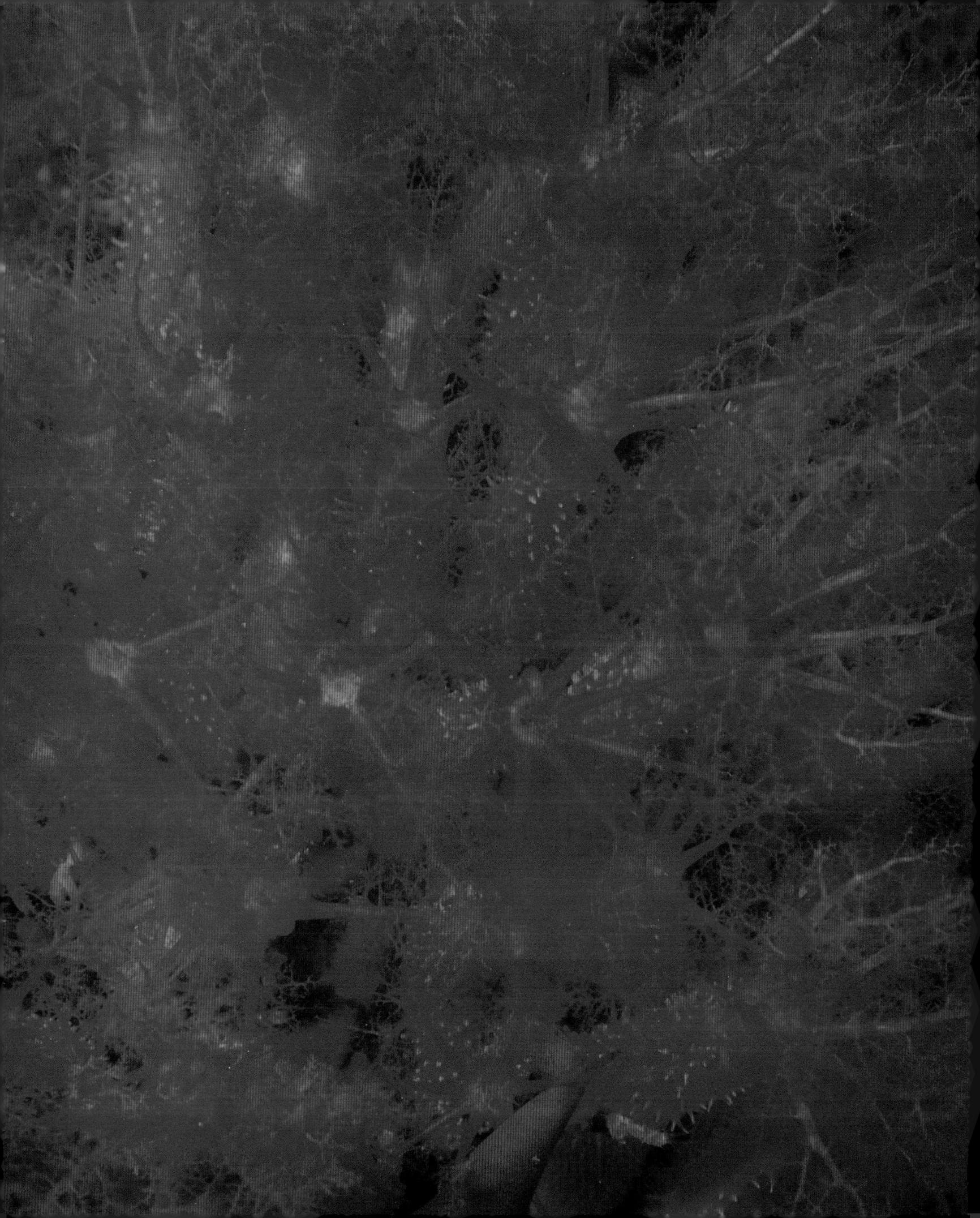

FIORDLAND UNDERWATER
New Zealand's Hidden Wilderness

PADDY RYAN & CHRIS PAULIN
PHOTOGRAPHS BY PADDY RYAN

© 1998 Patrick Alan Ryan and Christopher David Paulin

© Copyright 1998 Exisle Publishing Co. Ltd.

All rights reserved.

ISBN 0-908988-10-9

First published 1998 by Exisle Publishing Ltd

PO Box 8077, Symonds Street, Auckland 1035, New Zealand.

Ph: 64-9-303 3698; Fax: 64-9-309 0191.

e-mail: mail@exisle.co.nz Website: http://www.exisle.co.nz

Design by C. Humberstone.

Photographs by Paddy Ryan.

Additional photographs by Chris Paulin, Lance Shaw and Gilbert van Reenen.

Artwork by Streamline Creative Ltd, Auckland.

Printed in Hong Kong by Colorcraft Ltd.

This book is published with the assistance of The New Zealand Lottery Grants Board,
whose support is gratefully acknowledged.

All rights reserved. No part of this publication may be reproduced or transmitted in any form or by any means, electronic or mechanical, including photocopying, recording, or any information storage or retrieval system, without prior written permission from the publisher.

This book is dedicated to our children
Sarah and Lucy Ryan
David, Thomas and George Paulin
and to the children of New Zealand.

Acknowledgements

THIS book would not have been possible without the assistance of many people who freely and willingly provided us with information, assistance and advice, commented on the manuscript, and drank our beer. We thank all those listed below and any others we may have inadvertently overlooked.

In particular colleagues at the Museum of New Zealand Te Papa Tongarewa: Clive Roberts and Andrew Stewart (Fishes), Bruce Marshall (Molluscs), Wendy Nelson and Glenys Knight (Algae), Rick Webber (Crustaceans) and John Yaldwyn (Crustaceans and other marine invertebrates), and at the National Institute of Water and Atmosphere (NIWA), Alistair MacDiarmid (Crustaceans), Steve O'Shea (Octopods), Chris Battershill (Sponges and Ascidians), Dennis Gordon (Bryozoa), John Booth (Crustaceans), Karen Miller (Corals), Helen Rotman (Echinoderms), Geoff Read (Worms) and Dick Singleton (Brachiopods).

Special thanks to Ken Grange (NIWA), without whose enthusiasm, support and knowledge of the fiord ecosystems, this book would never have appeared. Fortunately for us, he was too busy to write it and despite our trampling all over his 'patch', Ken supported us to the hilt during its production. Jeanette Watson of Melbourne (Hydroids) assisted with night diving and was polite enough not to comment on the lack of a camera in the housing. Trevor Willis (Leigh Marine Laboratory), collector of the first specimen of *Fiordichthys slartibartfasti*, enthusiastically assisted in the field (more so when his drysuit didn't leak) and provided moral support throughout the project by continuing to laugh at our jokes (he also drank more than his fair share of our beer).

Staff and students from Otago University's Department of Marine Science, especially Brian Stewart, Euan Harvey, Nadine Parker, Franz Smith, Craig Loveridge and Wayne Jacobs, provided invaluable assistance in the field and allowed us to include many of their fiord ecology research findings in this book.

Individuals from other organisations also assisted with information from their various fields of expertise. Ian Stewart, Kathy Walls and Lindsay Chadderton, Department of Conservation; Cameron Hay, Cawthron Institute; Peter Johnson, Landcare Otago; Tony Brett and John Clausen, Ministry of Agriculture and Fisheries; Rob Mattlin, Victoria University; Carol Gardner and Dave Wilson, Te Anau Wildlife Park; John Steffens, Irene Barnes, Malcolm Anderson and other Guardians of Fiordland's Fisheries provided useful information on fisheries issues.

Len Cobb of Cobb-Horwood Publications, publishers of the excellent *The Story of Fiordland National Park* (in association with the Department of Conservation), generously gave us permission to base our diagram and description of the Life-cycle of Te Namu the Sandfly (page 162), on the one in his book.

Logistical support in the field was provided by Bob Walker (*Renown*). Lance Shaw and Ruth Dalley (*Evohe* and latterly of the *Breaksea Girl*) enthusiastically supported this project and shared their years of Fiordland experience. Kathy Jamieson and Dick Moore (*Pembroke*) also provided good company and sound advice.

Ian Hamilton, Alistair Childs and Chris Richards of the Milford Underwater Observatory introduced us to their new facility, and were positive about our book from the start. Graeme Back and Leigh Stevens of the Milford Hotel (since renamed Mitre Peak Lodge) assisted us with accommodation, for which our thanks.

Finally, we would like to express our appreciation with special thanks to the New Zealand Lottery Grants Board, which generously provided funding to enable the research for and publication of this book.

(Frontispiece) **A massed group of strawberry holothurians feeding in the weak tidal currents of Long Sound, Preservation Inlet.**

(Overleaf, page 5) **Exposed estuary at the head of Milford Sound.**

(Overleaf, page 8) **Mitre Peak, Milford Sound. Fiordland's steep mountain walls continue underwater to the floor of the fiords.**

(Below) **Many small islets at fiord entrances are remnants of glacial sills.**

Contents

Acknowledgements 6
Introduction 10
Fiordland's Marine Environment 14
Conservation Issues 20
Seaweeds 26
Sponges 36
Coelenterates 44
Worms 60
Brachiopods 68
Molluscs 74
Crustaceans 84
Echinoderms 94
Bryozoans 112
Ascidians 116
Fishes 124
Other Marine Vertebrates 142
Topside Biota 152
Research 164
Human Impact 170
Environmental Management 178
References 186
Glossary 188
Index 189

Introduction

FIORDLAND in remote south-west New Zealand is renowned for its awe-inspiring alpine and coastal landscapes and dramatic climatic regime. The interaction of mountains and water in a landscape shaped by ice has attracted visitors for centuries. However, although the terrestrial environment has been extensively explored, the marine environment has until recently remained a hidden wilderness.

Chris Paulin's great-grandfather Robert Paulin wrote a book on Fiordland, which was pubished in 1889. *The Wild West Coast of New Zealand – A Summer Cruise in the Rosa* became part of family folklore. Chris developed an interest in retracing some of his forebear's footsteps. His chance came in 1993 during a Museum of New Zealand field trip to the southern fiords. I was fortunate to be invited to join the group.

Robert Paulin was evidently a rugged type. He began each day of his stay in Fiordland with a swim around the boat. We weren't that enthusiastic. On our first swim we were well insulated with wetsuits.

We slipped into the chilly dark brown water with a certain amount of reluctance. I was blasé about diving in tropical waters but a little apprehensive about this daunting environment. Chris was more sanguine: he'd trained during winter in Wellington Harbour and at least knew what to expect from temperate diving. With my bias toward warm water diving, I was not optimistic as it didn't seem possible that anything I might observe would warrant getting cold in poor visibility water.

That first dive in Dagg Sound confirmed all my prejudices. It was cold, the visibility was limited, there was a strong surface current and I saw little of interest. So much for diving in Fiordland, I thought. Back on the boat I contemplated my next dives with even less enthusiasm. The afternoon dive near the outer coast involved an altercation with a weight belt and massive swells that mercilessly buffeted me and my camera housings. Chris watched with a certain amount of amusement as I struggled to refit my slipping weight belt. He didn't enjoy the dive either.

The third foray into the waters of Fiordland redefined diving for me. The visibility was at least 30 metres, an eagle ray leisurely glided past, schools of butterfly perch swam in and out of the forests of *Macrocystis*. I surfaced totally exhilarated, bubbling with enthusiasm for the Fiordland diving experience.

The Fiordland magic followed thereafter on a daily basis, right up to the end of our fish-collecting exped-

ition. It is difficult to imagine, but it goes something like this. You jump into oily brown cold water, bob around at the surface and exchange signals with minders on the boat.

After clearing the dive plan for the final time you swim the ten metres separating you from the near-vertical wall of the fiord. Here you purge your buoyancy compensator and head down into the murk. Somewhere between five and ten metres you burst through the oily interface between the 'freshwater' and salt water layers and into a realm of clear green water. Above, a strange yellow-brown light filters down as if you are in a sepia photograph from the 19th century.

As you level out and adjust buoyancy to the new depth, shadowy white shapes emerge at the limit of vision. Come closer and they are revealed as black coral colonies. Just to confuse you, they are a brilliant white. Your torch reveals colonies of bright pink hydrocorals. Every vertical face exposed to the weak tidal currents is covered with life, while other areas appear virtually barren.

Most of the organisms you see are sessile, which is to say they can't move around. Bright red brachiopods mingle with orange and yellow sponges. White sea-urchins hang by tube feet off impossible cliff-faces, seeking out a feed of organic matter. On suitable perches, claret-coloured featherstars spread their arms to glean microscopic plankton from the water.

Where there are flat ledges with silt or sand deposits, a different set of creatures flourishes. Elegant tube

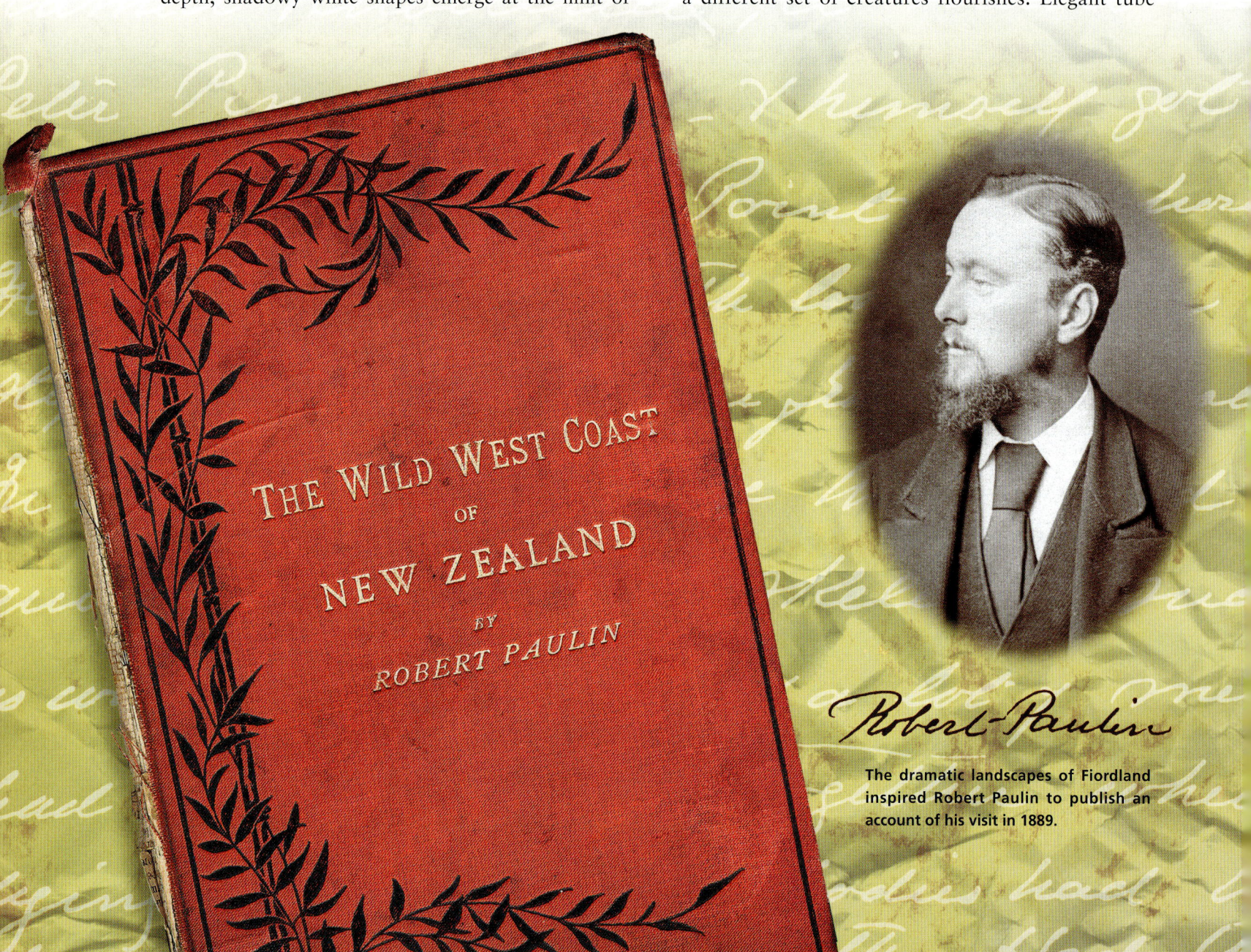

The dramatic landscapes of Fiordland inspired Robert Paulin to publish an account of his visit in 1889.

anemones flutter their tentacles in the slight current, feather duster worms extend their elaborate gills, and opal fish move in disconcerting spurts of sand. From time to time you encounter a branch from the forest above or a dead black coral colony. Every available space is seized by sponges or compound ascidians. They appear to drip, ooze, and cascade off their dead host.

Throughout this plenitude is a plethora of fishes, taking advantage of the rich biomass. Butterfly perch, jock stewart, scorpion fish, blue cod and a variety of triplefins are everywhere. The triplefin numbers must be seen to be believed. In some places the rocks can barely be discerned under a squirming layer of fish. In the northern fiords the occasional southern splendid perch brightens up an already spectacular dive.

At depths of 20 metres or more, sea pens thrive. At night they may luminesce and if touched gently, respond with a ripple of tiny blue flashes. Suddenly, a juvenile fur seal will blast in for a closer look and swim away, making you wonder if it was an illusion.

You exit from this fairyland back up through the cold brown freshwater layer, which washes the salt out of your dive gear for you. Towering above you are the glacier-gouged cliffs of the fiord, dense with vegetation. Apart from the muted background noises of the dive boat, the only sound is the liquid burbles of a bellbird. Magic. I'm now a born-again temperate region diver and it was Fiordland that made me see the light, or more accurately, the murk. And with true New Zealand understatement, Chris has occasionally been heard to mumble that his dives in Fiordland weren't too bad.

Hence this book. We both believe that Fiordland underwater is just as worthy of preservation as the Fiordland above water. It seems strange to include from the mean high tidemark upwards in Te Wahipounamu, the South West New Zealand World Heritage Area, and leave out everything below the waterline.

It is our view that this extraordinary realm is under threat. Commercial fishing and crayfishing exert pressure on most of the fiords, while Doubtful Sound and Milford Sound come under stress from the large number of tourists and recreational fishermen.

We've been relatively vociferous on the issue. Often we feel we are preaching to the converted, while the sceptics say to us "prove it... show us that this is a unique environment worthy of preservation." Fortunately for us, the New Zealand Lottery Grants Board had an interest in our project. The Board generously gave us a grant to facilitate the research and enable the publication of this work.

We hope that the evidence presented in this book on Fiordland's underwater environment will lead to greater awareness of its fragility and concern for its long-term conservation.

Our more modest aim is that *Fiordland Underwater: New Zealand's Hidden Wilderness* will prove a useful reference and at least help to allow sound decisions to be made.

Paddy Ryan
Greymouth, 1998

Chris Paulin
Wellington, 1998

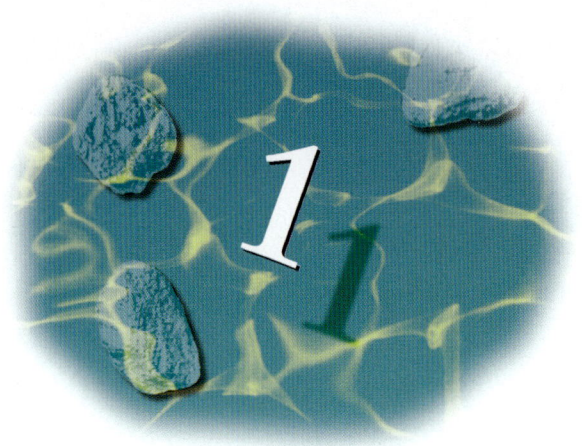

Fiordland's Marine Environment

FIORDLAND'S marine environment is unique, becoming known internationally for its spectacular and fragile biodiversity (Grange 1990).

Although Fiordland is New Zealand's largest national park, the fiords themselves, which make up 1872 kilometres of the coastline (SRC 1993), are excluded from the protected area. There are 15 main fiords, with an average length of 21 kilometres. They are sheltered by steep mountain walls rising to heights of 2000 metres or more, extending over 200 kilometres from Milford Sound southwards to Preservation Inlet. The fiords were formed by the drowned lower reaches of valleys that were occupied by glaciers during the last glacial period, approximately 20,000 years ago.

The marine ecosystem within the inner fiords is unlike any other on the planet. At the fiord entrances and the exposed rocky coast, the ecosystem and marine biodiversity is typical of southern New Zealand, similar to that found in coastal waters of Otago, Southland and Stewart Island. Habitats within the fiords vary considerably but are all dominated by the unique environmental conditions.

At the head of the fiords, small areas of stony estuaries, often clogged by numerous logs and branches swept down by floods, form the few areas of flat habitat.

The remainder of the fiords are characterised by near-vertical rock walls which plunge several hundred metres to the fiord floor, with only limited narrow ledges and shelves. Throughout the fiords innumerable waterfalls create a surface layer of freshwater over the seawater, while near the entrances the remains of glacial sills, debris left from the retreating glaciers, form an effective barrier, restricting seawater circulation into the fiords. The combination of species living within the fiords, from warm, cold and deep water habitats, is found nowhere else.

The fiords are famous for their spectacular scenery and high rainfall. Fiordland is one of the wettest places on earth; however, few areas in the rugged terrain serve as catchment basins, so an hour of rain transforms the forested fiord walls into white water cascades that plunge hundreds of metres to sea level. Under normal conditions, the dense forest prevents erosion, so the volume of sediment carried by freshwater run-off to the fiords is

(Right) **Milford Sound with Mitre Peak at left. Fiordland's glaciated topography and massive freshwater run-off are important factors contributing to the unique ecosystem found below the waterline within the fiords.**

low. Sedimentation rates in the fiords roughly equal those on the continental shelf several kilometres from land. As the freshwater runs through the forest, it picks up decaying vegetation, along with humic acid that stains it en route to the fiord, so that it resembles weak black tea or beer. During and after extreme rainfall the water becomes more like milky tea. In one dive in Milford Sound we encountered a freshwater layer 16 metres deep, which cut off all light from reaching the seawater below.

In most estuaries, winds, waves and currents mix the inflowing freshwater with the higher density salt water. In the fiords, these forces are reduced, so there is little mixing of the two layers. As a result, a variable layer of yellowish-brown, practically freshwater, overlies salt water. This layer ranges from the 16 metres mentioned above, down to half a metre. The layer becomes thinner towards the mouth of the fiord.

Continual water run-off causes the freshwater surface layer to flow out of the fiords, carrying with it small quantities of salt water. Seawater flows from the ocean into the fiord beneath the surface layer and replaces that lost. This process is known as estuarine circulation. This deeper current is weak but it carries deep water larvae into the fiords from the adjacent ocean, where the continental shelf is extremely narrow. This allows species normally found in deep water to enter the fiord environment. Elsewhere the wide margins of the continental shelf prevent this from occurring. Many of these species can live only in habitats with low levels of food, light and sedimentation, together with weaker currents and waves.

In effect Fiordland is a vertical, rather than horizontal estuary. The freshwater layer prevents the vertical colonisation or migration of totally marine organisms. Salinities within the top few metres fluctuate, depending on the amount of rain. Neither freshwater organisms nor true marine species can survive and the organisms are thus estuarine. Only triplefins, shrimps, barnacles, blue mussels and in summer, green sea lettuce, typical of estuaries, live in this layer. The transition to the marine environment generally ends at around five metres depth, where the clear seawater stays a relatively constant temperature year-round.

The surface water layer both filters and absorbs light. The amount of light at 10 metres typically equals the amount at 70 to 100 metres off the open coast. The spectral quality of the light that penetrates is changed by the surface layer. Selective light filtration by the yellowish-brown surface layer allows only greenish light, the least suitable wavelengths for photosynthesis, to penetrate. Perhaps because of this, seaweeds do not usually flourish in the fiords further than a few hundred metres from the open coast. Forests of seaweeds rarely become established and phytoplankton populations are low most of the time.

The fiord ecosystem relies mainly on imported plant material which comes from the surrounding forest. Periodically, landslides cause trees on the steep mountainsides to fall into the fiords and these provide a direct terrestrial link to the marine food chain. These landslides leave spectacular scars on the fiord wall but are rapidly recolonised by forest. After they sink, the trees become covered by sea-urchins, burrowing teredo molluscs and grazing snails that can eat away, in less than a year, a beech tree trunk that is 10 metres tall and one metre in diameter (Grange and Goldberg 1992).

(Left) **White sea-urchins *Pseudechinus huttoni*.**

(Right) **Most marine life within the fiords is found within the top 40 metres of the cliff walls.**

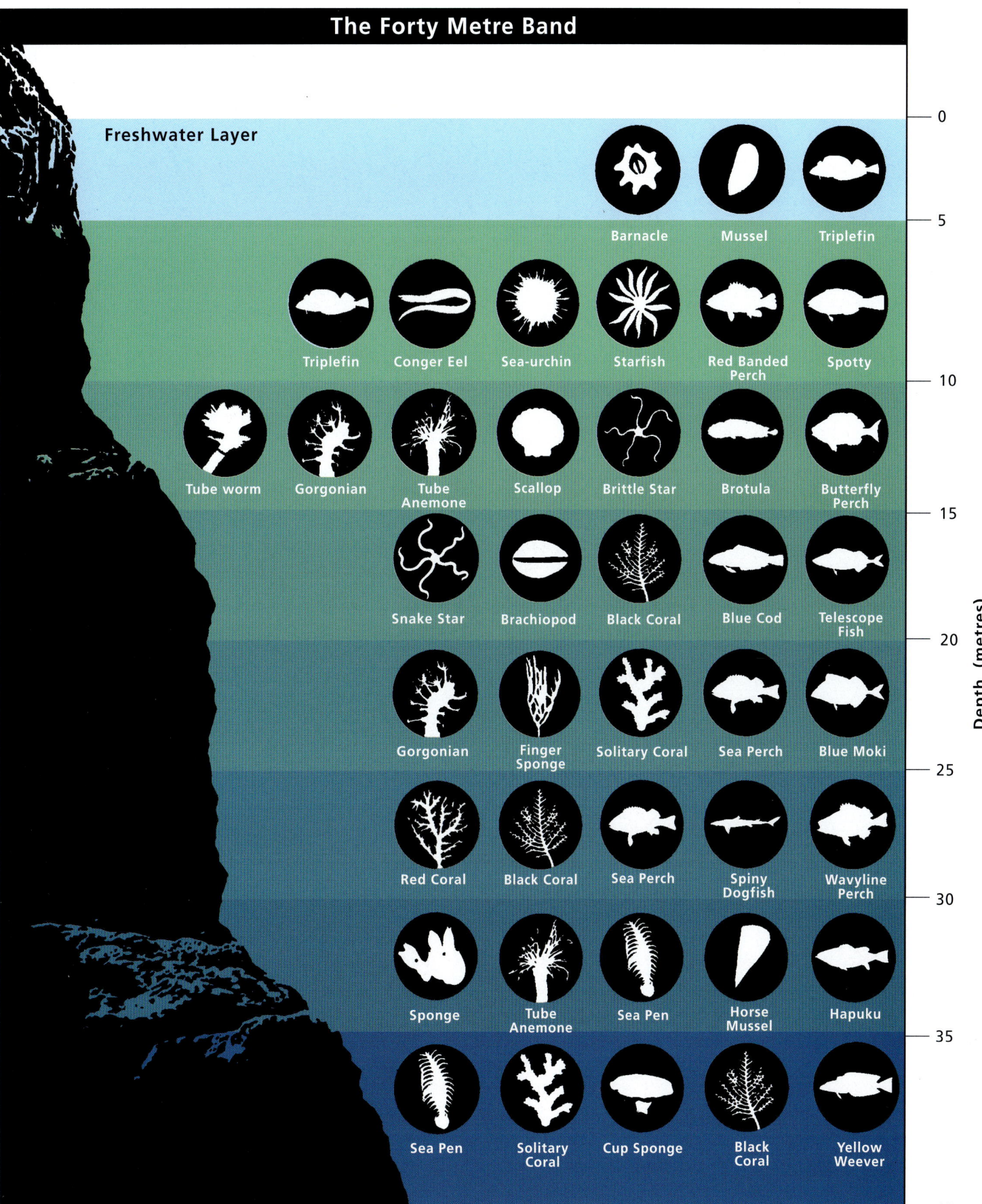

FIORDLAND'S MARINE ENVIRONMENT

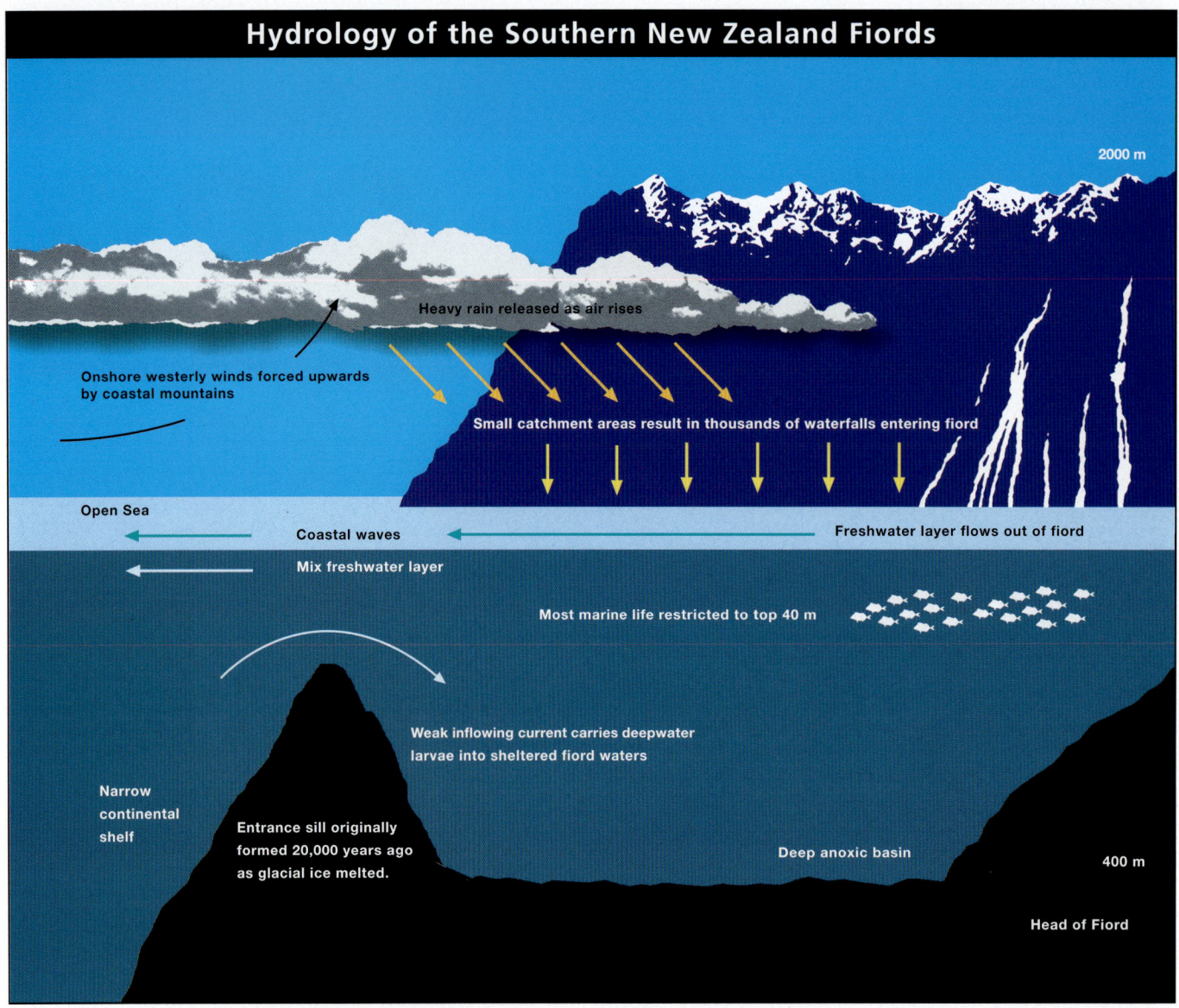

The marine community includes many species believed to live only in the fiords and even those species collected elsewhere may exist here in greater abundance and at shallower depths. Up to 1998, over 180 species of fish and several thousand species of invertebrates and algae have been recorded from the area (Museum of New Zealand Te Papa Tongarewa and National Institute of Water and Atmosphere unpublished databases and biodiversity surveys).

Many of the animals that live within these communities are long-lived, slow growing, extremely sensitive to increased sedimentation as they feed by catching small plankton or filtering water, and live attached to the rock walls in a colourful mosaic of tubeworms, colonial sea-squirts, anemones, hydrocorals and other inver-tebrates.

Franz Smith (1995) found a high average diversity in species-rich areas. This was over twice the average diversity found elsewhere in similar latitudes. Brachiopods, or lampshells, dominate the invertebrates, just as they did in the ancient seas. Elsewhere they are now restricted to a few specialised environments where they don't have to compete with faster growing, more adaptable species.

The South Island fiords contain eight species and represent the most diverse and abundant populations of brachiopods in existence (Lee, in McCrone 1994).

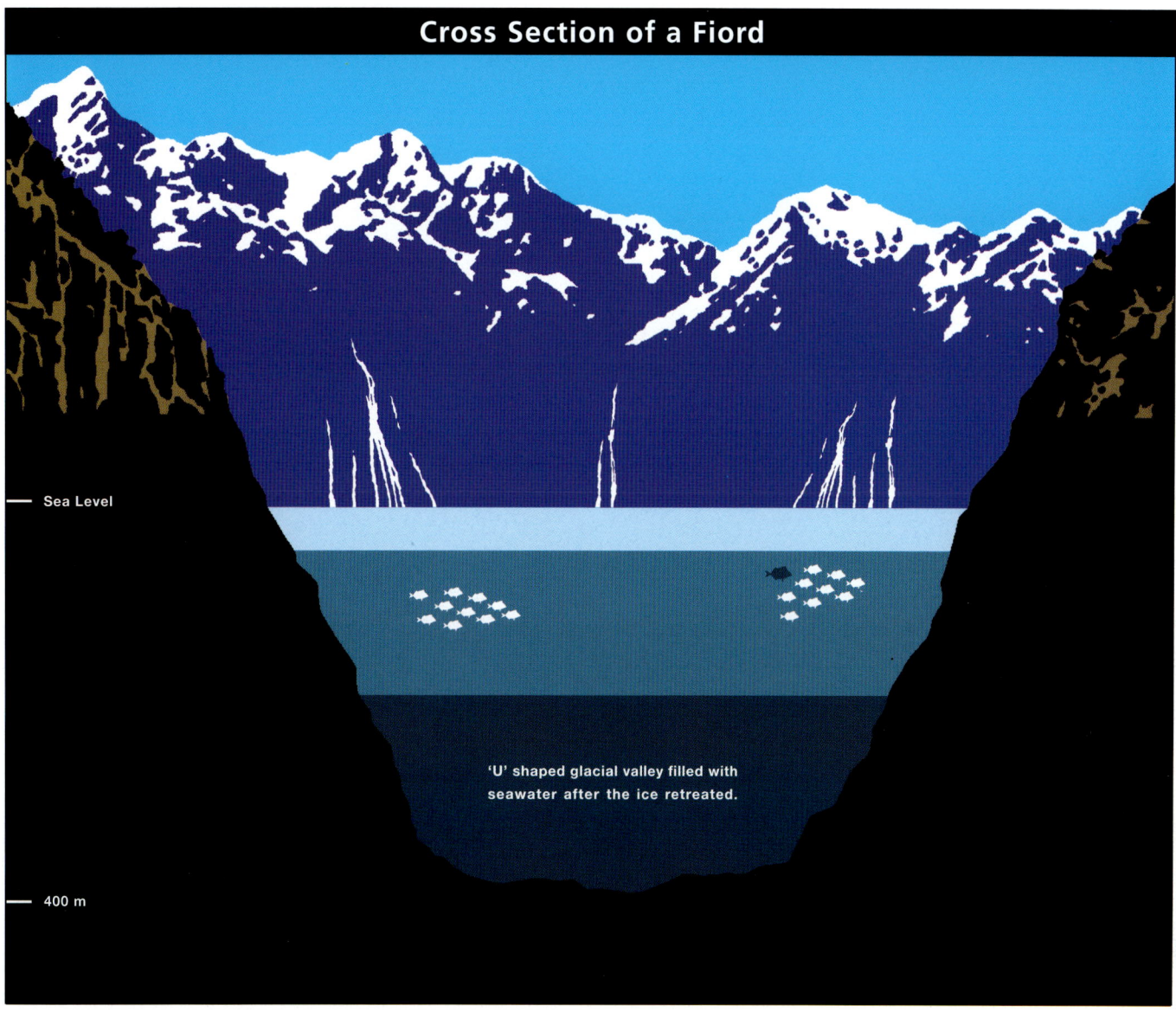

Cross Section of a Fiord

Sea Level

'U' shaped glacial valley filled with seawater after the ice retreated.

400 m

Large colonies of the antipatharian black coral occur throughout the fiords as shallow as three metres, with maximum abundance between 15 and 20 metres. Black corals generally live only around offshore islands, in very clear water and seldom shallower than 40 metres. The density of black corals in the fiords averages one colony per 3.5 square metres, giving an estimated total population of over seven million colonies within diving depths. These range in size from tiny bushes to trees over five metres tall, often covered by encrusting species (Grange, in McCrone 1994).

A small population of the protected bottlenose dolphin *Tursiops truncatus*, is resident in Doubtful Sound (Williams 1992). The environment here contrasts in almost every way with other areas where populations of bottlenose dolphins have been studied, due to the closed nature of the fiord, cool water temperatures and the extreme changes in salinity.

A combination of physical and biological processes, including unusual patterns of climate, terrestrial vegetation, topography, oceanography and larval recruitment, creates a unique environment. The marine communities in the New Zealand fiords are found nowhere else along the New Zealand coast, nor do they occur in fiords in other parts of the world.

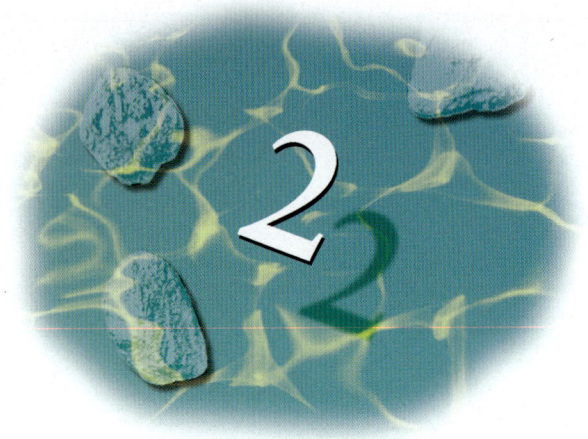

Conservation Issues

MOST of Fiordland's residents and visitors would no doubt agree that this unique environment must be protected. The most difficult aspect of this is the question: just what is it that requires protection and what is the problem?

Management issues have already been addressed in other parts of New Zealand where large areas of coastline act as a buffer, enabling the spreading out and diluting of human activities. However, Fiordland's inner sounds have an extremely restricted and fragile environment that is limited to an estimated 40 square kilometres, less than half the size of some of the country's larger harbours.

Elsewhere in New Zealand, fishing pressure, both commercial and recreational, has had a serious effect on some species and access to remaining stocks is often hotly debated, while environmental issues such as pollution are well understood, if not largely resolved. The Fiordland marine environment is vulnerable: it exists in its pristine state today because of its isolation.

Concerns arise from the increasing ease of access and paucity of information available. One example is the recreational fishing activities. Daily bag limits for recreational fishermen, while effective in other regions, may be too high for the limited stocks within the fiords.

The increase in the number of tourist vessels has increased the amount of sewage being discharged, while noise pollution from numerous vessels and aircraft detracts from the wilderness environment. This activity may also affect bottlenose dolphin populations that use the inner fiords as nursery areas, and disturb breeding colonies of seals and seabirds.

Introduced seaweeds and other organisms in ballast water is a concern, especially if proposals for export of freshwater proceed. Sedimentation in Doubtful Sound may be a problem with the extra tailrace proposed, but the extent of any impact is unknown: it may affect only a small area. A more serious sedimentation problem may be caused by the introduced Australian possum, which is now spreading into even the most remote fiords. The devastation these browsing mammals have on the native vegetation is likely to dramatically increase the number of tree-slips.

Other potential threats, which have all been proposed at various times, include future tourist developments, increased fishing pressure, both targeting of additional

(Right) **Deepwater Basin at the head of Milford Sound provides a sheltered anchorage for the fishing fleet.**

species (which may be key components of the ecosystem), bioprospecting for anti-cancer chemicals, building of oil rigs, mining, dredging, and sewage disposal.

Many of these problems may be no greater than in other areas of the New Zealand coast; others may be catastrophic. Until additional baseline information is available it will be impossible to determine the resilience of the fiord ecosystem.

Commercial fishermen are well aware that tossing rubbish such as beer cans overboard, increases the habitat for predators that feed on their crayfish stocks. In 1992 a commercial users' 'Code of Practice' was introduced; this was followed by a code for recreational users (*Beneath the Reflections*) in 1996.

The fishing industry has long recognised the problems: marine reserves are one potential solution. The industry was instrumental in establishing the two marine reserves in Fiordland in 1993, and in 1995 it participated in setting up the Guardians of Fiordland's Fisheries, work-

(Left) **Tree-slips contribute plant matter to the marine ecosystem. Browsing by introduced mammals damages the protective forest and may significantly increase the number of slips.**

(Opposite, Top) **Cray pots and fishing gear stored alongside the jetties at Milford contrast with pristine environment.**

(Opposite, Lower) **Anchors can accidentally destroy black coral colonies that may be 300 or 400 years old.**

(Overleaf, Left) **Crayfish (rock lobster) are targeted by both recreational and commercial fishermen.**

(Overleaf, Right) **While sea kayaking is considered to be low impact ecotourism, all human visitors to this region pose a potential risk for the fragile environment.**

CONSERVATION *23*

ing with the Ministry of Fisheries to describe the fish stocks and identify the fisheries issues which need to be addressed. The two marine reserves established are insufficient to protect the fiord habitat. In 1990 seven areas were identified as the minimum requirement.

The establishment of two reserves, however, has focused diver attention on those areas and damage has increased – small marine reserves are counterproductive. Fisheries management techniques appear to be sustaining and protecting the commercial fish stocks and can also address the recreational fish catch. Yet these regulations are aimed at controlling long-term fisheries, rather than enhancing environmental protection.

Commercial harvesting of the Fiordland marine ecosystem is an integral part of the ecology of the area. Human activities, both extractive and non-extractive, must be included in the management of the area. There is a need for a co-ordinated management plan which could include marine reserves, controlled fisheries and supervised access. The Department of Conservation, Ministry of Fisheries, regional councils, the tangata whenua, commercial users and other national and local groups will all have a role to play in this management plan (see Chapter 18).

Many of these problems stem not from poor management but from the lack of information. Sadly, Fiordland's marine environment may be too fragile to allow continued procrastination in addressing these issues.

The major purpose of this book is to collate existing knowledge and present it in a manner which allows more people to make an informed input. It took a hundred years from the publication of Robert Paulin's book *The Wild West Coast of New Zealand*, to the setting up of the South West New Zealand World Heritage Area Te Wahipounamu. It should not require another century for Fiordland's underwater realm to receive the respect it is due.

3

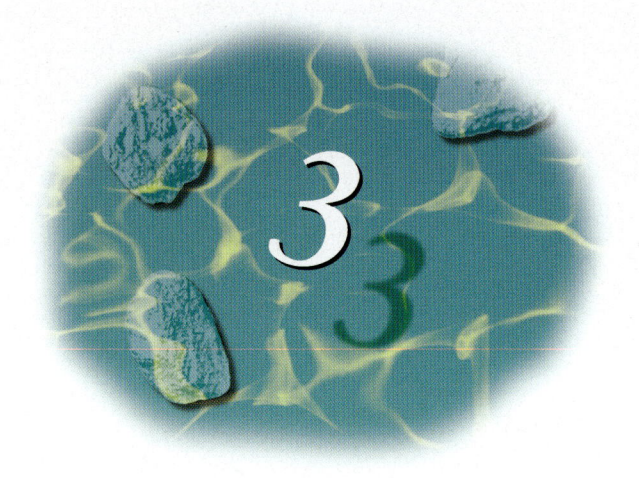

Seaweeds

THE subtidal environment of the fiords is characterised by the absence of large areas of macroalgae which dominate the temperate reefs of New Zealand. Here in Fiordland, algae are restricted by two environmental factors: the freshwater layer, which reduces available light for photosynthesis, and the steep topography, which prevents algae establishing holdfasts on the vertical faces. Although large forests of algae do not dominate, algae are present in suitable places, particularly towards the middle and outer fiords. The fiord entrances support dense algal beds characteristic of southern New Zealand and the outer exposed coasts are well covered with bull kelp *Durvillaea* spp.

There are two principal groups of marine algae: macroalgae which are classified as red, green and brown seaweeds, and microalgae (mainly diatoms) which form the phytoplankton. There are many groups represented in the microalgae: diatoms, dinoflagellates, nephiolophytes, chrysophytes, and others. In most marine ecosystems the algae form the base of the food chain. However, in the fiords the freshwater layer reduces light levels, although primary production is still high. This role is supplemented by vegetative matter falling from the fiord walls.

Although there has been some survey work carried out, as with most other groups of Fiordland organisms, the seaweeds and their ecology are as yet poorly understood. The flora is rich and diverse, yet it is extremely sparse, with very low biomass in some areas. There are strong differences between the inner, sheltered zone and the outer, more exposed zones of the fiords. Algal diversity is as high as in other regions, but both biomass and diversity decrease towards the heads of the fiords and often only a few individual plants are present. Phytoplankton are present in the fiords and during periods of reduced run-off these can cause blooms as the light increases.

Many algae species are tolerant of changing salinities in the surface freshwater layer, but are unable to become established on the steep rock walls. *Wittrockiella lyallii* is commonly found in shaded upper intertidal areas. Urchins, which graze on seaweeds, cannot survive in the freshwater layer and a strong, but narrow band of perennial brown seaweed is found at the low water mark, for example *Carpophyllum flexuosum, Sargassum sin-*

(Right) ***Enteromorpha* sp., *Adenocystis utricularis* and sea lettuce *Ulva* sp., dominate in sheltered sandy and rocky intertidal areas in outer Chalky Inlet.**

clairii, *Cystophora* spp., and towards the outer coast *Durvillaea* spp. Some algae can tolerate a wide range of salinities and the intertidal-freshwater layer is dominated by algae including sea lettuce *Ulva lactuca*, and others such as *Stictosiphonia vaga*. This algae-dominated shoreline is progressively replaced by barnacles towards the outer fiords. Much of the soft shore areas at the head of Milford Sound are dominated by the filamentous brown alga *Pilayella littoralis*, the red alga *Gracilaria chilensis* and the green sea lettuce *Ulva lactuca*.

Below the intertidal-freshwater layer is a four to five-metre band dominated by sea-urchins where coralline algae are prolific, and seasonal perennials, like *Ulva*, are common but low in density and patchy. In less steep areas, there are often *Caulerpa brownii*, *Ralfsia* (a crustose brown alga), *Carpophyllum*, and below these extensive beds of *Ecklonia* and *Carpophyllum flexuosum* to depths of 23 metres. Often these species are found in Fiordland at depths greater than elsewhere in New Zealand, and in some fiords, such as Caswell Sound, large individual bladder kelp *Macrocystis pyrifera* plants can be seen growing alongside black coral. *Macrocystis* is arguably the world's fastest-growing plant with daily increments of up to half a metre. Also in these depths leafy reds (*Hymenena*, *Rhodymenia*, *Stenogramme interrupta*) and branched red *Champia* can be found growing on stones in the sand beds, with an increase in diversity southwards.

Below the intertidal to depths of four metres algae dominate the fiord walls, particularly in summer when light levels are higher. Towards the mouths of the fiords, intertidal *Ulva* and Neptune's necklace *Hormosira banksii*, and other subtidal algae, *Enteromorpha*, *Rhodymenia*, *Pilayella*, together with margin weed *Marginariella boryana* and *M. urvilliana*, form a distinct band with blue mussels. The transition zone below the freshwater interface is characterised by bare rock with branching velvet *Codium fragile* and coralline turf algae which are grazed by sea-urchins and other species which

(Left) *Arthrocardia wardii*, a red algae, is found with other algal species in a dense band below the intertidal zone.

(Below Left) Crustose coralline algae cover much of the steep rock face. Correct species identification relies on microscopic characters.

(Opposite page) Bladder kelp *Macrocystis pyrifera*, rarely forms dense algal forests within the fiords, but individual plants are relatively common.

SEAWEEDS 29

migrate up during times of decreased run-off as salinities increase.

In depths below this, typical light levels at 15 metres are equivalent to 65 to 90 metres in the open coast and there are very few plants. In places there may be solitary *Macrocystis* plants.

On the outer exposed coasts where strong wave action disrupts the presence of sea-urchins and breaks up the freshwater layer, many deep inner fiord dwelling algal species (*Cystophora platylobium, Ecklonia radiata*) are found in shallower water. The warmer waters within the sounds enable many northern species, usually found in warmer waters of northern Westland or Marlborough, to be present alongside southern sub-Antarctic species.

The southern flora is similar to that of Stewart Island. Algae are more dominant towards the south although diversity does not increase. This may reflect the presence of larger, more obvious species and the less steep topography where more habitat is available, as well as the temperature regime. *Ecklonia* in the north is gradually replaced by *Marginariella* and *Cystophora* in the southern fiords. *Macrocystis pyrifera* is present in large belts in the south and reaches a northern limit around George Sound. The massive bull kelps *Durvillaea* spp, are restricted to the outer coast or entrances to the fiords where wave action breaks up the freshwater layer. Their distribution also wanes to the north, until only small patches are present at Milford. However, this alga is common at other sites further north. *Durvillaea* grows up to five metres high with fronds up to ten metres long. These broad flattened blades are supported on a short bare stipe (or stem) arising from a conical holdfast. The blades of *Durvillaea antarctica*, unlike *D. willana*, have an internal bouyant honeycomb tissue resulting in a wide drift dipersal by ocean currents to places where they do not grow. The tough outer skin is pliable and rubbery, unlike the internal honeycomb tissue which is easily separated. Because of this, *Durvillaea* fronds were used extensively by Maori to make strong bags and sandals for use when exploring the coastal areas.

Nancy Adams reported three adventive species, *Polysiphonia brodiaei*, from northern Europe, and *Champia affinis* and *Sargassum verruculossum*, both from South Australia, have become established in Fiordland. The impacts of these alien species need to be carefully monitored. Although there are a number of adventive species recorded from various parts of New Zealand, this is not just a recent problem associated with ballast water. Adams, in her excellent book on New Zealand seaweeds, notes that several adventive algal species have sporadic distributions or are confined to harbours that were frequented by whalers and sealers in the 19th century.

(Right) **Individual *Ecklonia radiata* plants may be found alongside extensive beds of sea rimu *Caulerpa brownii* in outer fiord areas.**

(Below) ***Durvillaea* stipes support fronds up to 10m long.**

(Right) **Neptune's necklace** *Hormosira banksii* occurs subtidally and in the lower intertidal zone in outer fiord habitats. This distinctive algae is confined to Australasia and in sheltered areas may form beads up to 20 mm in diameter.

(Opposite, Top Left) **Flexible flapjack** *Carpophyllum flexuosum* forms dense beds in the outer southern fiords, while smaller individual plants are found towards the inner fiords.

(Opposite, Top Right) *Codium* sp. This genus is characterised by the velvety or spongy texture of the plants. Their growth form ranges from prostrate cushions to erect branched species.

(Opposite, Lower Left) **Bladder kelp** *Macrocystis pyrifera* may grow to 20m in height and is found in colonies in sheltered offshore waters.

(Opposite, Lower Right) **The paddle weed** *Ecklonia radiata* is more common in the northern fiords of this region. The single stem expands into a wide, flattened blade with lateral lobes.

SEAWEEDS 33

(Right) *Zonaria turneriana* and *Carpomitra costata* are typically found in sheltered subtidal areas near the outer fiord entrances.

(Opposite) *Carpomitra* is a widespread genus represented in New Zealand by a single, highly variable species *C. costata*.

(Below) The margin weed *Marginariella urvilliana* grows up to 2m or more, gradually replacing *Ecklonia* in the southern fiords.

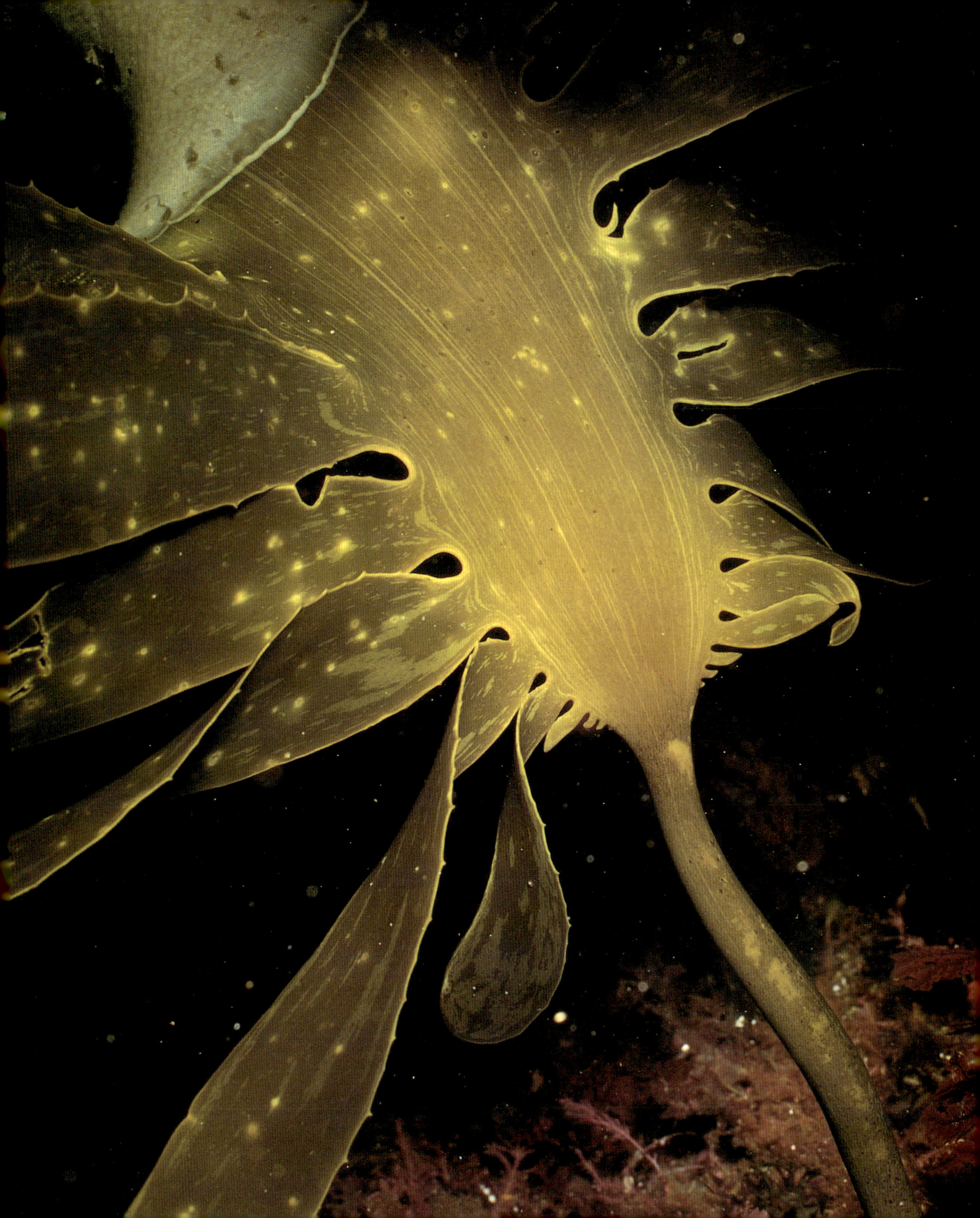

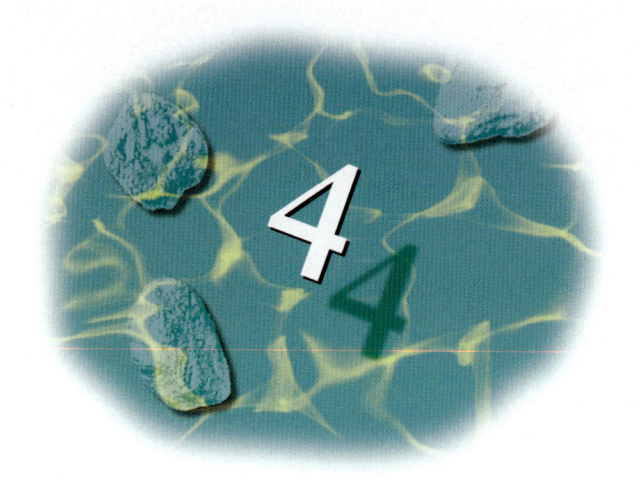

Sponges

OVERALL, the biota of Fiordland's cliff walls and ledges may seem as diverse as most other rocky reef regions of temperate New Zealand, and indeed it is on a par with reef communities worldwide. At any one location below five metres depth, however, the walls can appear quite barren of life. Apart from rocky promontories or pinnacles, where water movement is accelerated, most of Fiordland's reef walls remain unoccupied by noticeable encrusting animals. Vast regions of cliff wall can be covered by patches of thinly encrusting coralline algae and there are significant areas of unoccupied space.

Encrusting invertebrates do not make up a large biomass in Fiordland. Sponges in particular seem to be present in limited numbers and reduced diversity within any one fiord. This situation contrasts markedly with the densely-packed sponge-dominated communities found outside the fiords.

A collection of subtidal marine invertebrates and algae was made throughout Fiordland in 1991. Of 195 species identified, 50 species were sponges but in any one fiord, fewer than 13 species were found in any significant numbers. The reasons remain obscure, as there seems to be adequate food of the size ranges taken by sponges (picoplankton and organic particles). Where sponges do occur they are certainly conspicuous as they frequently crowd around black coral trees and most display vibrant colours. Their distribution remains patchy and even the most crowded community characterised by sponges supports a low biomass.

The sponges found in Fiordland have affinities with warm temperate, deep water and even subtropical species. For these reasons, Fiordland is an extremely interesting place for sponge research. According to New Zealand's leading sponge expert Chris Battershill (NIWA), these sponges represent almost all the major groups of sponges and occur in a variety of shapes, from thinly encrusting forms through massive forms and erect branching morphologies.

The only group not represented are the stony sponges or Sclerosponges, which is not surprising as they are an ancient group and extremely rare. The fact that each of the three other groups is represented is significant. These groups are the demosponges, calcarea and hexactinellids or glass sponges. The latter group is usually found only in very deep regions of the sea and in polar regions.

(Right) **Golf ball sponge** *Latruncalia*, **new species. Sponges grow in a wide variety of shapes and may be thin and encrusting or massive cushions, tubes, fingers, or round.**

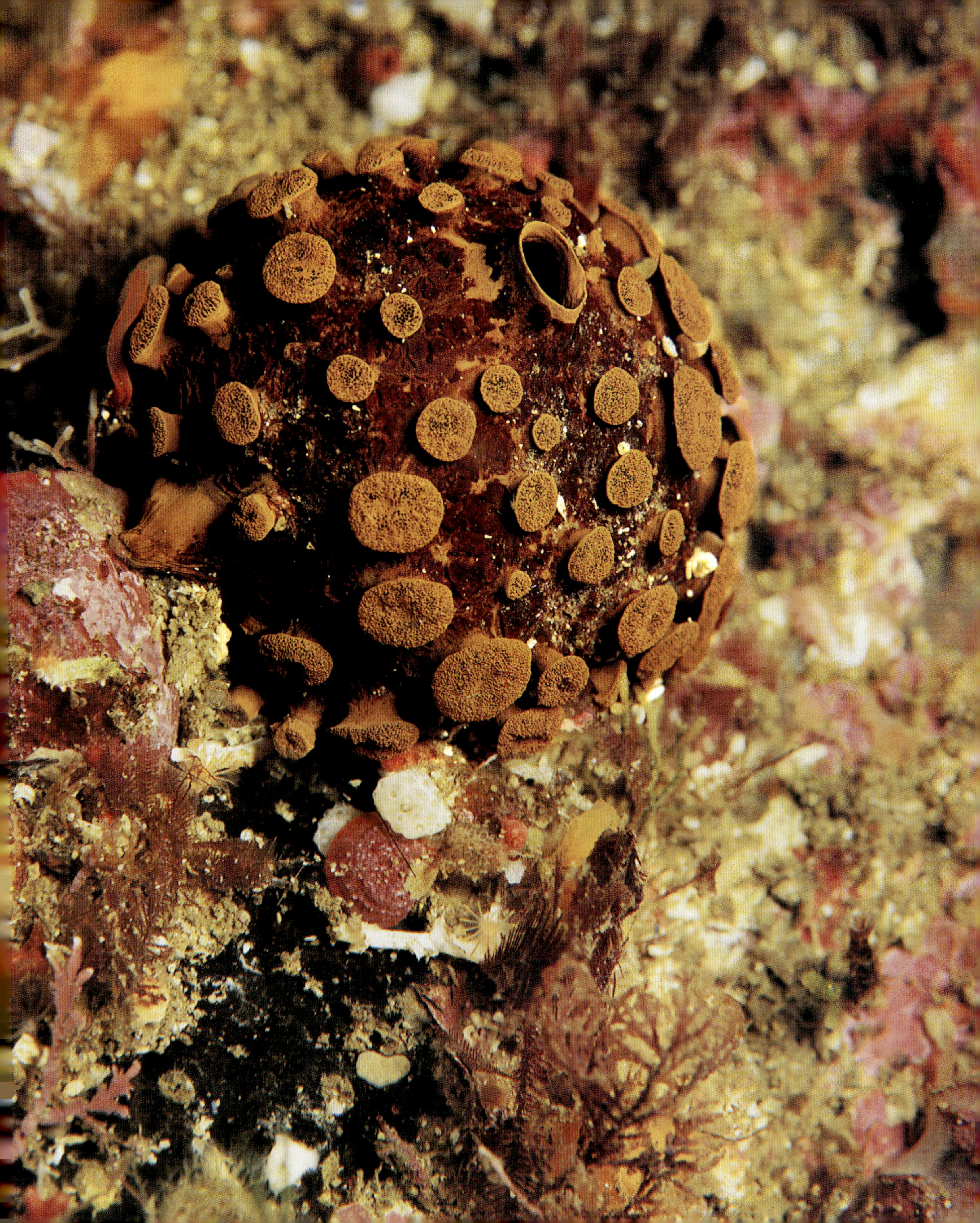

Fiordland is unique in that a hexactinellid sponge *Symplectella rowei*, is found inside the fiords and perhaps of even more significance is the fact that it occurs in diveable depths (30 to 50 metres) on the cliff walls of Doubtful Sound. Individuals of this species can grow to very large size, easily the largest sponges in Fiordland. They offer a remarkable opportunity for study.

The demosponges are the largest sponge group and are well represented in Fiordland in terms of the orders found. Most species are common around New Zealand's coasts and only a few seem to be endemic to the Fiordland area. These include a verongiid and an axinellid, both as yet undescribed and possibly new. The commonest species is the distinctive cup or ear-like axinellid sponge *Axinella tricalyciformis*, which is the only species to occur in abundance in all the fiords. This is usually a deep water species, not found within diving depths elsewhere. Other common species are the haplosclerids *Callyspongia ramosa* and *Callyspongia latituba*, tall finger sponges with *C. latituba* characteristically growing as tubes or pipes; thinly encrusting Poecilosclerid species such as the yellow *Aegogropila* sp. and species of *Mycale*, which can spread as large patches; and the massive green hadromerid sponge *Latruncalia brevis*.

The calcarea are also present throughout Fiordland, abundant in some areas. These sponges are characterised by possessing calcareous, not siliceous, spicules. The most common of the eight species found was *Clathrina coreacea* which looks like candyfloss on the cliff walls. Also reasonably abundant was the flask-like *Leucettusa lancifer*. Chris Battershill notes that a number of calcareous sponges were found which were not readily identifiable.

Sponges are not significant species in terms of the ecology of Fiordland submarine reef walls. They occur in patches commonly associated with dense aggregations of black coral, which in turn appear to be associated with areas of strong water movement. In most instances, sponges will be growing on the coral trees, as opposed

(Left) **Limited dispersal** is a feature of asexual reproduction and clusters of genetically identical individuals, such as this group of tube sponges, can be found in scattered locations throughout the fiords.

(Opposite page) **Golf ball sponges** reproduce asexually by 'budding' off small colonies.

SPONGES 39

In other areas of coastal New Zealand, sponges are often confined to shaded areas or deeper water by dominating algae; however, in the lower light levels within the fiords, sponges compete successfully at much shallower depths:

(Right) *Raspailia topsenti*.

(Opposite page) *Raspailia* sp.

40   FIORDLAND UNDERWATER

to occupying the seemingly abundant bare space on the rock walls. This phenomenon could be a function of some limiting factor in the food supply, where every opportunity must be taken to be positioned in strong current. It could also reflect potential competition with coralline algae which grows very well in the subdued light of the fiords.

The overall lack of diversity and biomass of sponges may partly be a function of the limited powers of larval and asexual propagule dispersal known to be a feature of sponge reproduction. Where a species is found, there is usually a small enclave of conspecifics and given the prevalence of asexual reproduction in most sponges, it is highly likely that satellite individuals will be clones or buds from an original settler.

Once established, sponges may exist unaltered in number or size for considerable periods of time. Their size reflects an optimum for prevailing conditions and should those conditions deteriorate, the sponges will shrink. There are not many sponge predators, hence loss of individuals is rare. Nudibranchs eat sponges and leatherjackets will also predate them when very hungry, but will seldom eliminate a whole animal. The only major source of mortality is infection from marine pathogens and there was evidence in the 1991 survey that some populations had recently succumbed to a fungal attack. This is not an uncommon event during the summer months in any marine ecosystem.

Fiordland's sponges are unusual in that they are limited in their diversity and generally do not grow well. Although they are being investigated for bioactive compounds, which may be used in new and potentially lucrative anti-cancer drugs, the impoverished fauna minimise the potential for a sustainable harvest. Huge quantities of specimens may be needed to yield a few milligrams of chemical: in one case 2400 kilograms of sponge from the Indo-Pacific produced just one milligram of chemical.

(Right) **Breadcrumb sponge *Polymastia croceus*.** This and other sponges from Fiordland are under investigation for their potential anti-cancer properties.

(Below Right) **Zoanthids** are able to exploit any available substrate and colonise grey cup sponges.

(Below) **Unidentified orange tube sponge (Family Haplo-scleridae).**

(Opposite page, Top Left) ***Callyspongia latituba*.** The tall growth form of finger sponges enables this organism to intercept food particles higher in the water column.

(Opposite, Top Right) ***Thorecta* new species.** Many undescribed sponges are found within the fiords and are the basis for ongoing research.

(Opposite, Lower) **The grey cup sponge *Axinella tricalyciformis* is the only sponge species which occurs in any abundance within the fiords.**

SPONGES 43

5

Coelenterates

CORALS, hydroids and their close relatives the sea anemones, are coelenterates. Most are similar in structure with a stalked body and a circular mouth surrounded by a disc of stinging tentacles. Each individual animal, or polyp, may range in size from microscopic to several centimetres across. Food is collected by the stinging tentacles, which then pass it to the central mouth.

Anemones, corals, soft corals and gorgonians abound in Fiordland's sheltered waters: Ken Grange describes the fiords as New Zealand's coelenterate heaven, with many new species awaiting identification. More than two dozen species of coelenterates have been recorded within the fiords. Many of these are usually considered deep water species.

On steep current-swept rock walls black corals *Antipathes fiordensis*, solitary corals *Monomyces rubrum*, *Desmophyllum cristigalli*, and *Caryophyllia profunda*, fan-shaped soft corals and gorgonians such as the orange-yellow *Acanthogorgia breviflora*, and anemones compete for space with millions of other sessile organisms. On the sediment-filled ledges the most obvious organism is the tube anemone *Cerianthus* sp. This pale tentacled anemone grows inside a parchment-like tube which may be up to 100 millimetres high and 40 millimetres across and is found from 10 metres depth, particularly in areas of fine sediment. In other parts of the world the tube contains a variety of freeloaders, other animals which share the parchment cylinder. Whether these are parasites or commensal is not yet known.

In the deeper waters of 18 to 35 metres that scuba divers can reach, five species of sea pen have been recorded. At the marine reserve in The Gut, the sea pen *Sarcophyllum* sp. can be seen. This spectacular orange organism can grow to 200 to 250 millimetres high and 100 millimetres across when fully extended. If it is gently handled it produces a faint blue bioluminescence but it requires a dark day for this to be seen, even at the low light levels at which it is found.

Colonies of black coral *Antipathes fiordensis* are the visually dominant feature of the underwater. Named for the appearance of the dead skeleton, the live colonies appear an eerie white against the deep blue-black fiord waters. Although usually found only below 40 metres in clear oceanic waters around islands, black coral colonies grow in Fiordland waters as shallow as four metres. This

(Right) Red coral *Errina novaezelandiae*, occurs at depths of 25 to 30m, but may be found in waters as shallow as 6m in the southern fiords.

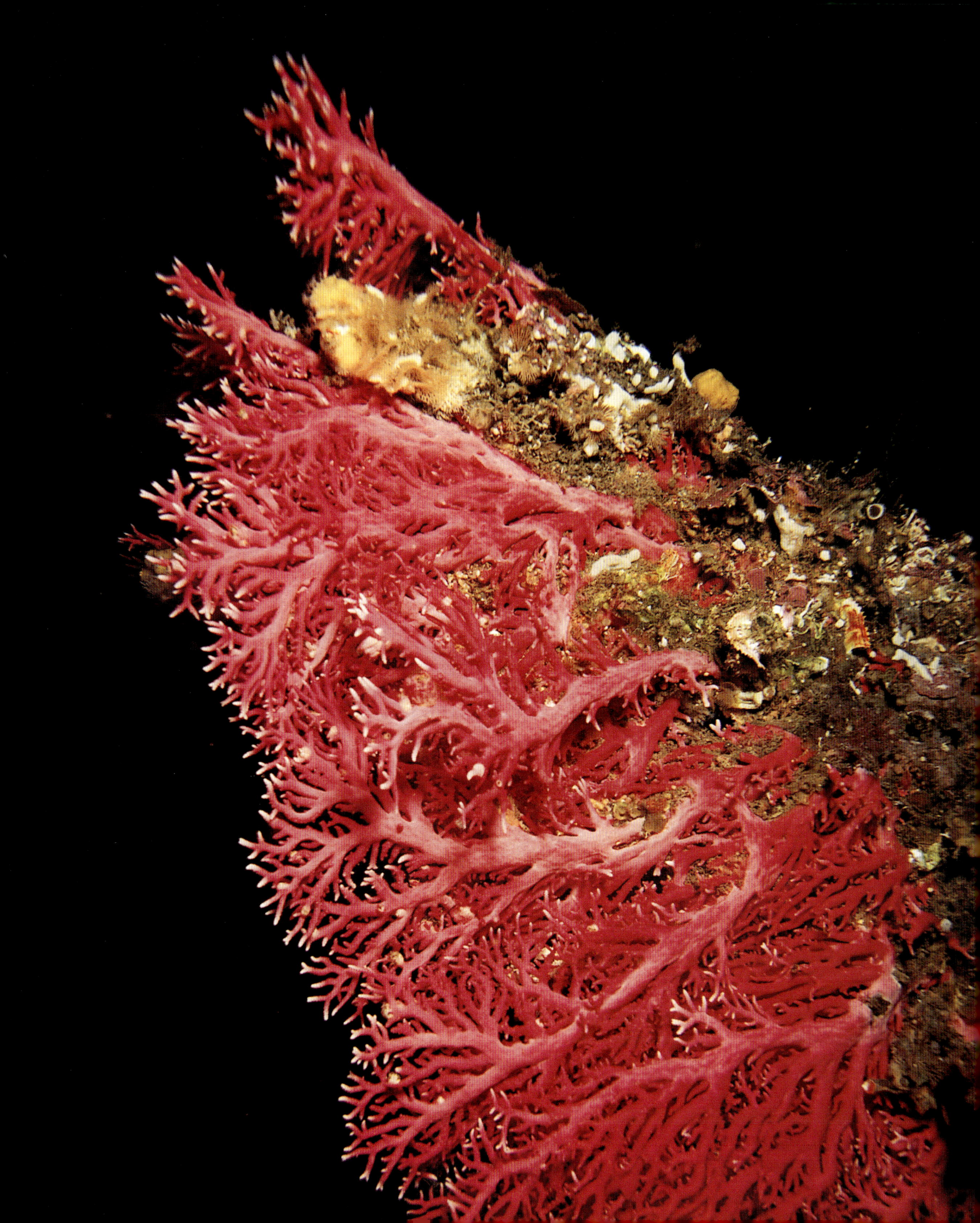

(Above) **Black coral *Anti-pathes fiordensis*** is normally found only around offshore islands, at depths below 40m. Its presence in Fiordland waters indicates the unique environmental circumstances found here.

(Right) **Sea pens *Sarcophyllum* sp.** are found at depths of 25 to 30m in the northern fiords.

(Opposite, Top) **A second species of *Sarcophyllum*** is found in the southern fiords.

(Opposite, Lower) **Secondary polyps on the upper part of the sea pen** collect food and pump water in to keep the colony turgid.

46 FIORDLAND UNDERWATER

provides an invaluable and unique opportunity to study a species which otherwise would be virtually inaccessible.

The density of colonies throughout the fiords has been calculated at one colony per 3.5 square metres, indicating that throughout the fiords there may be as many as seven million colonies ranging in size from minute bushes to large trees four metres tall. Research by Ken Grange has shown that most colonies are found between 15 to 30 metres, but they have been seen as deep as 100 metres by utilising a ROV (Remotely Operated Vehicle).

Each colony has its own epiphytic fauna: smaller colonies may have only a few snakestars, while larger ones are scattered with snakestars, crustaceans, sponges, even the small white sea-urchin *Pseudechinus* on occasion, while schools of butterfly perch *Caesioperca lepidoptera*, congregate in and around the branches.

The perching snakestar *Astrobrachion constrictum* is found only on black coral and virtually every colony supports its own population. This is a fascinating example of a symbiotic relationship where both the coral and the snakestar benefit. During the day the snakestar remains tightly coiled on a branch, protected among the stinging cells of the coral, but at night it extends its arms and waves them through the coral, stealing food collected by the polyps and at the same time clearing debris which otherwise would potentially smother the colony. Black corals also develop defensive sweeper tentacles that are used to attack epifauna that settles on damaged portions of the colony, and could if unchecked, eventually overgrow the colony.

Growth of black coral is slow, even by coral standards. Ken's measurements on tagged colonies show an increase of 1.5 to 25 millimetres per year. As the corals are colonies, different parts may grow at different rates, and there is no theoretical limit to the age. It is thought that the largest colonies may be 300 to 400 years old. Several methods have been used to determine growth, from direct measurement, radiography of growth rings, population structure and chemical labelling of the skeleton. Natural mortality from biological causes is low; however, catastrophic environmental conditions can be significant. Heavy rain can cause the freshwater layer to increase,

(Right) **The unusual transparent starburst sea pen *Kophobolemnon* sp. is found at depths of 18 to 25m in Long Sound.**

(Lower Right) **Gorgonian corals can retract the polyps into the hard skeleton, while black coral polyps must cling to the exterior.**

(Opposite page) **Hydroid *Symplectoscyphus subarticulatus*. The fan-shaped colonial phase of many hydroids and other coelenterates is delicate and may be destroyed by the currents created by unwary divers.**

lowering salinity and threatening colonies in shallow water; too little rain decreases the surface layer, allowing more light to penetrate and triggering plankton blooms which smother colonies. The numerous 'tree slides' which occur regularly on the steep fiord walls appear to be the main cause of mortality and the largest colonies are found below stable hillsides or on underwater ridges or outcrops away from the path of landslides.

Current studies are attempting to unravel the reproductive strategy. Female colonies are obvious in late summer, and spawning has been observed close to full moon, but despite examination of hundreds of polyps throughout the year, males have only been recently discovered. Studies by Nadine Parker (1995) (University of Otago) and Karen Miller (1995) (NIWA) have shown that there is a 50:50 sex ratio in the coral and that it is a broadcast spawner, both eggs and sperm being released into the water column. It seems that previous studies missed the November to March timeframe, the only period when differentiation of the sexes underwater is possible.

Determination of the genetics of the population depends in part on the powerful tool of enzyme electrophoresis. Put simply, samples of body tissue are subjected to an electric field in a medium which allows the individual proteins to migrate and separate. Examination of the resulting traces allows subtle differences to be revealed. Karen's studies, based on this technique, have shown that around half of the colonies are genetically distinct, indicating sexual reproduction has occurred.

Results, however, indicate that larval dispersal is restricted both within and between fiords, therefore each fiord population has a separate gene pool. Karen also found that there were a substantial number of colonies which were genetically identical, some of which were in different fiords, separated by as much as 60 kilometres. This immediately raised a series of questions. Could broken-off pieces of colony be transported those sort of distances and reattach to the bottom? Karen considers this extremely unlikely and has suggested that the black corals may produce an asexual free-swimming planula stage. As yet no one has ever seen one of these, so it is a bold prediction, but one likely to be found true.

Elsewhere in the world, black coral is harvested commercially for the manufacture of jewellery and international trade is banned under the CITES (Convention on International Trade in Endangered Species) as black coral is regarded as an endangered species. In New Zealand, black coral is protected by legislation.

While only recently described, *Antipathes fiordensis* has been known for at least a century. Robert Paulin (1889) reported discovering a 'sea tree':

> A fine specimen of a sea tree was dredged up in this passage (Acheron) after our visit. The sea tree is a kind of seaweed which grows attached to rocks below the low-water line. It has branches, is hard and black as ebony, and in shape and appearance resembles a stag's horn.

Robert Paulin obviously saw the specimen long after the polyps had rotted away, leaving the black skeleton for which black corals are named.

A number of other species of coral are found in the fiords. These are also seldom seen as shallow elsewhere and include the large solitary corals *Desmophyllum cristagalli* and *Caryophyllia profunda*, several undescribed species of white, red and pink colonial stylasterine hydrocorals, the most common being red *Errina novaezelandiae*. Red coral, like black coral, is also protected by law and can be seen by divers below 20 metres depth, although many colonies may be found as shallow as eight metres.

While only scuba divers and snorkellers are likely to see red and/or black corals, non-divers can view these animals from the comfort of the Milford Underwater Observatory (see page 177).

Hydroids are small to medium-sized, plant-like colonies which grow on Fiordland's vertical reef system, but as yet have not been widely studied. The colonies usually consist of many thousands of tiny polyps, each living in its own cup, seated on the flexible, chitinous stems. All the polyps in a colony are connected throughout the colony by living tissue. Each polyp consists of a simple, sac-like body, surmounted by a mouth and a crown of tentacles. Being micro-carnivores, they capture small planktonic animals which are killed by stinging cells embedded in the tentacles. The prey is then passed to the stomach where it is digested. Digested food is shared by the entire colony.

Hydroids have a complex life cycle that includes a free-swimming sexual (medusoid or larval) stage and an asexual (colonial) phase. It is the colonial phase that is most often seen by divers and naturalists. When released from the colony, free-swimming medusae (tiny jellyfish) are too small to be seen by the naked eye.

Many hydroids protect their developing medusae or larvae in special, often beautifully sculpted chitinous receptacles attached to the colony. Hydroids have been studied in Doubtful Sound only from one collection made in April 1994, by Jeanette Watson of Melbourne, an authority on these interesting creatures. Diversity of species was found to be high throughout the Sound, although decreasing with distance from the ocean and below depths of 25 metres. This is because, being static predators, hydroids need good water movement to bring food to their tentacles and to disperse metabolic wastes; therefore there are fewer species and the colonies tend to be smaller in the more tranquil conditions near the head of the Sound.

Many of the species in the Sound are feather, or fan-shaped, or are composed of a network of stems jutting out from rock faces to take advantage of current flow. Hand-sized, tangled bright yellow colonies of *Sertularella robusta* grow on the tops of boulders to take advantage of the 'edge effects' of small increments in current flow. For the same reason, old black coral trees are a highly favoured substrate, especially for *Corhiza ritchiei* which clothes some coral trees in a lacy mantle of white.

Mussels growing just below the freshwater layer support thick colonies of two species, *Obelia australis* and a small *Hydrodendron*. Immediately below the freshwater layer the most abundant species is *Salacia buski* which grows in clusters of feathery, brown stems up to 150 millimetres high.

Deeper again, the brittle fan-shaped, honey-coloured colonies of *Symplectoscyphus subarticulatus* jut out from the rock. From the entrance to about halfway up the Sound, a small feathery white species, *Sertularia marginata* is common, usually growing on red algae. On reefs near the entrance, large yellow, bushy colonies of *Halecium beanii* grow on upward-facing rock surfaces.

(Left) **Black coral colonies are white; the skeletons black. This colony is festooned with snakestars.**

(Opposite Left) **Black coral colonies breed towards the end of summer, when the female colonies turn a distinctive pink-orange colour. Spawning probably occurs as a 'simultaneous' event but has not been witnessed.**

(Opposite Right) **Hydroid *Sertularella geodiae*. Sertuliid hydroids are characterised by the typically serrate appearance of the stalk.**

COELENTERATES

(Right) **Stalked anemones, like this unidentified white species, are often solitary, large and conspicuous.**

(Below) **The red anemone *Edwardsia* sp. camouflages itself by burying the stalk in sand or sediment.**

(Opposite page) **Anemones *Mimteridium cryptum* grow in dense colonies just below the freshwater layer.**

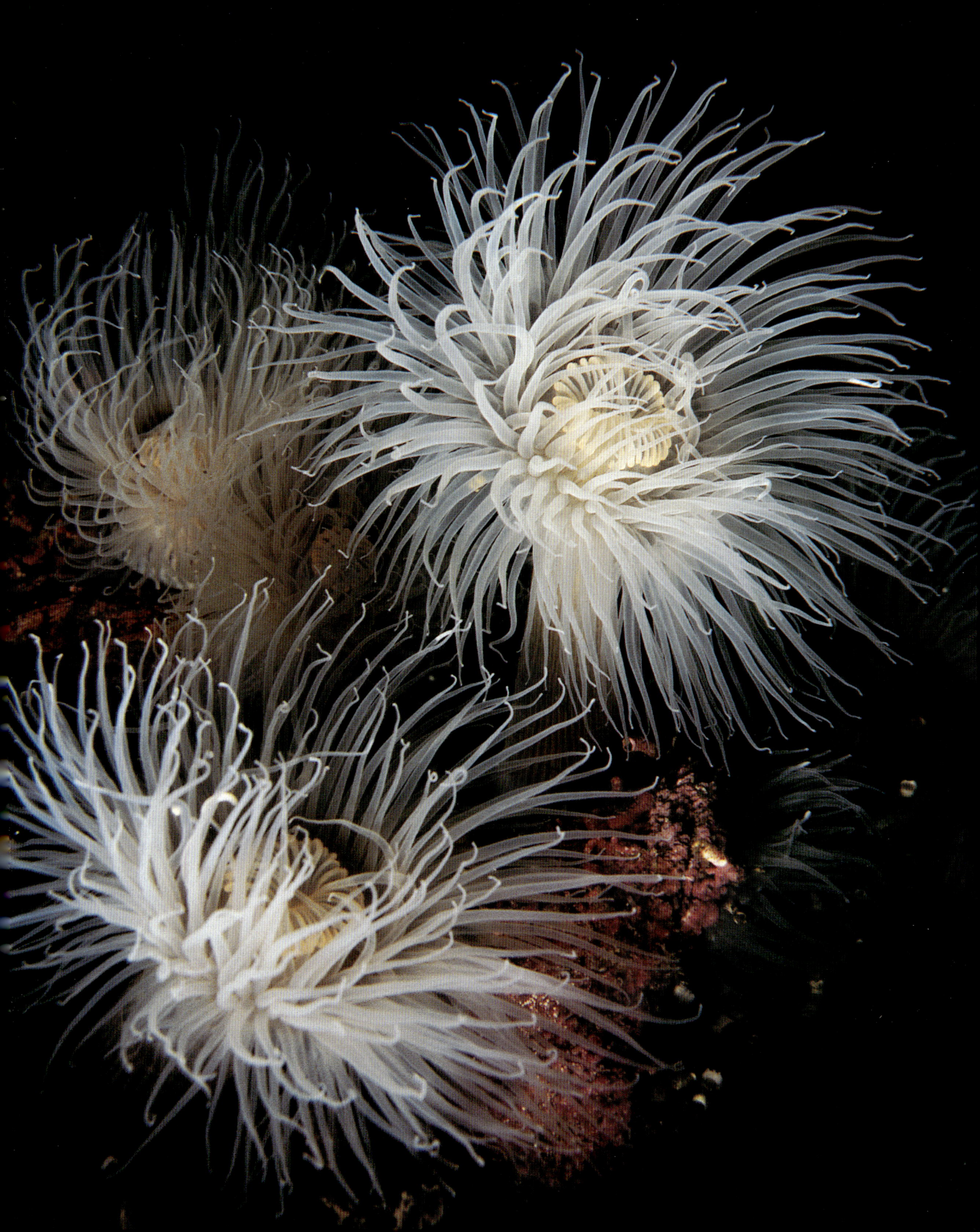

(Right) **Zooanthids *Parazoanthus* sp., are colonial animals usually found in deep water or in shaded caves and overhangs. They can also be seen at diving depths within the fiords.**

(Opposite, Top) ***Anthothoe albocincta*. Anemones have a mouth opening in the centre of the oral disc surrounded by a few to several hundred hollow tentacles.**

(Opposite, Lower) **The tube anemone *Cerianthus bollonsi*, can be observed on sediment-filled ledges throughout the fiords.**

COELENTERATES 55

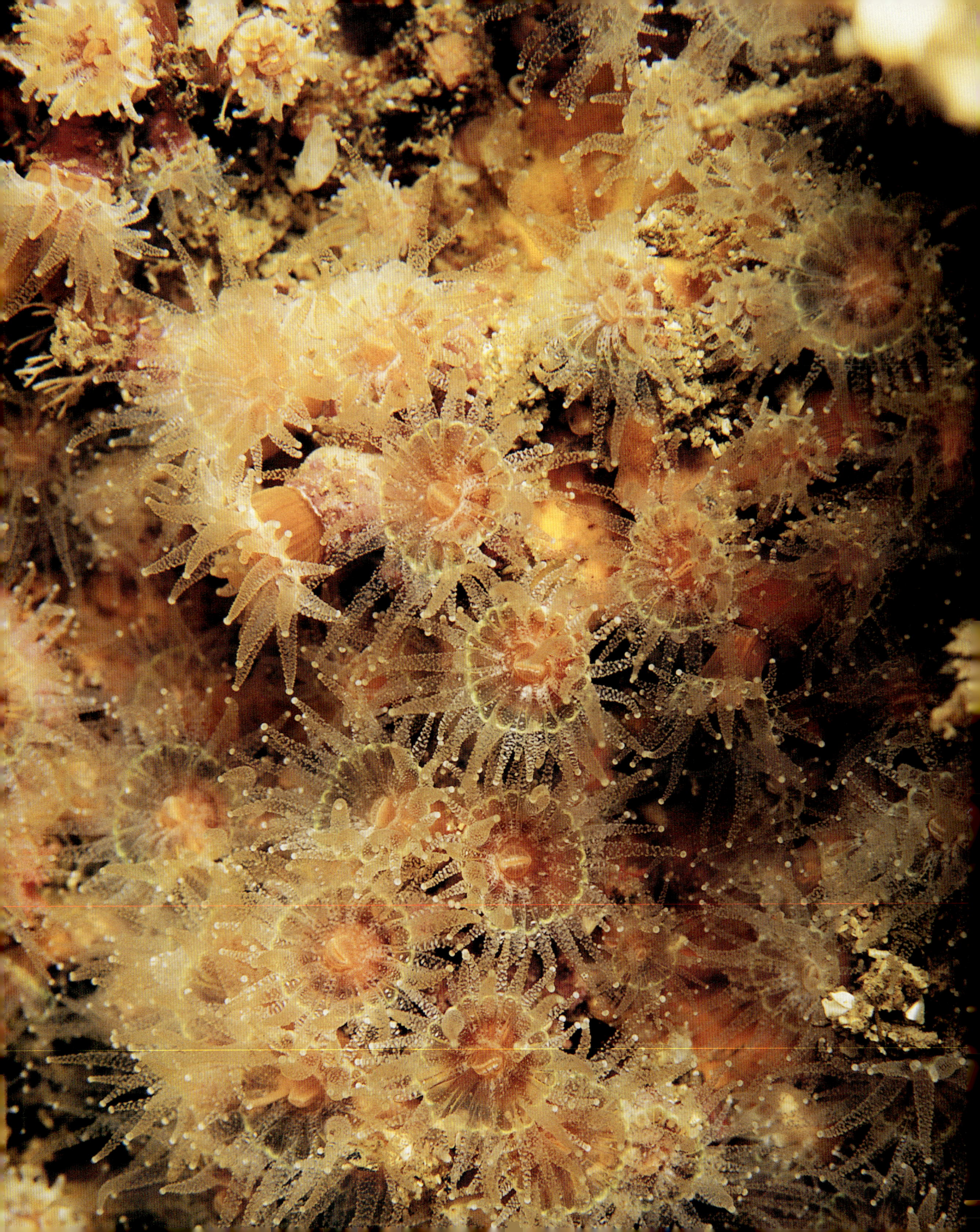

(Left) Stony corals *Caryophyllia profunda*, are closely related to the sea anemones but unlike these, they produce a calcium carbonate skeleton.

(Lower Left) The common cup coral *Monomyces flabellum* is found throughout the New Zealand coastline.

(Below) The octocoral *Alcyonium aurantiacum* is also called 'dead man's fingers' because of its form and colour.

(Opposite page) *Culicea rubeola*, a small colonial species of stony or sceractinian coral.

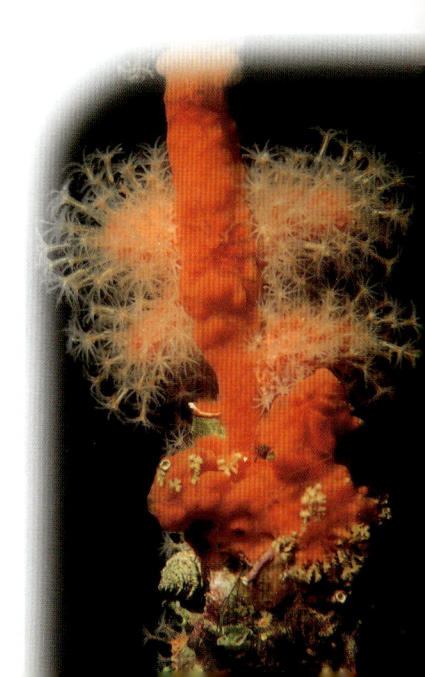

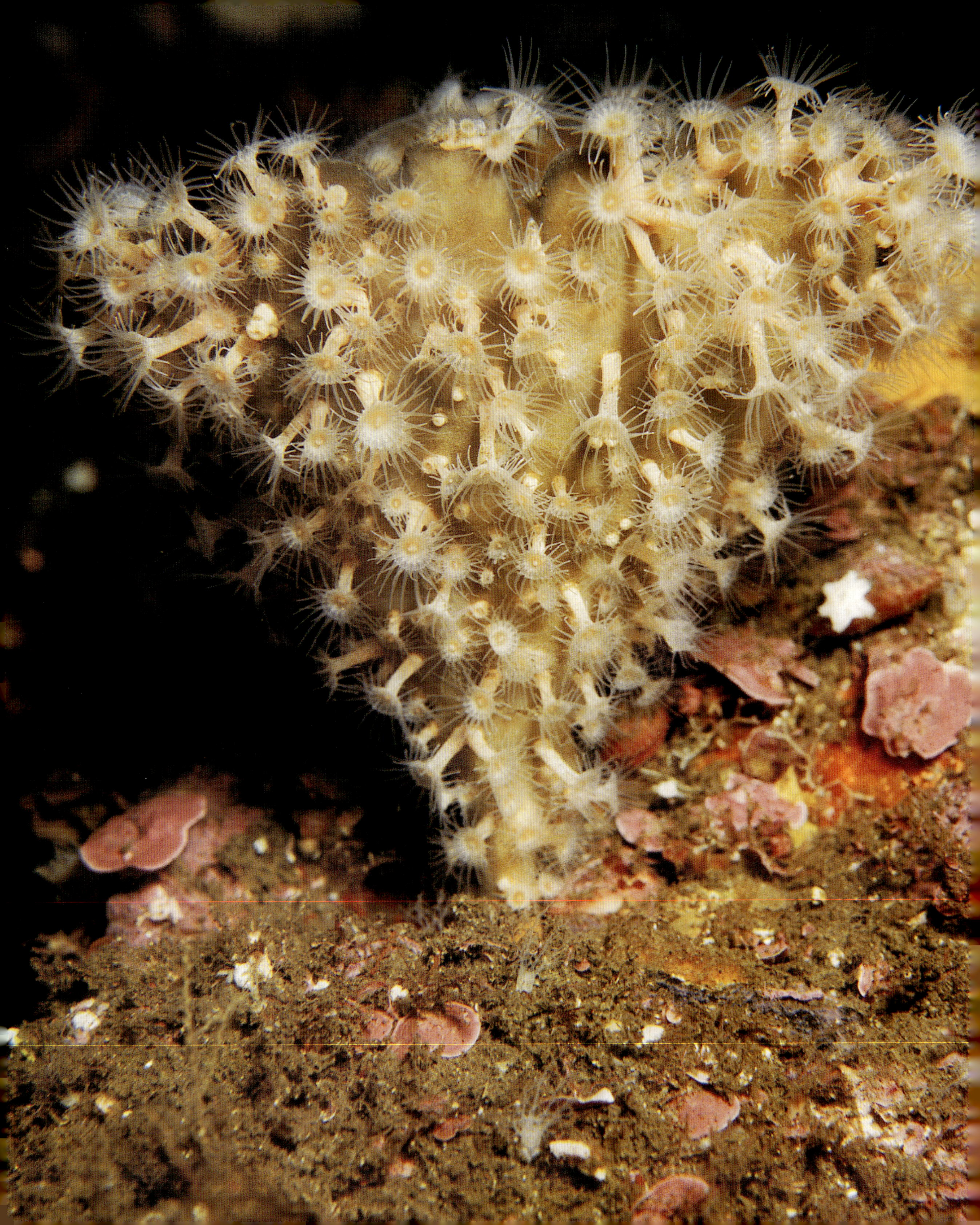

(Left) Octocorals, such as *Alcyonium aurantiacum*, are restricted to deep water over the continental shelf and the upper slope, except in Fiordland where they may occur as shallow as 5m.

(Below) *Culicea rubeola*, a colonial stony coral.

(Opposite page) White zooanthids covering a grey cup sponge.

6

Worms

THE term 'worm' is a catch-all, covering a vast range of different animal groups. Amongst the creatures loosely referred to as worms are flatworms, which belong to the phylum Platyhelminthes, the ribbonworms (phylum Nemertinea), the roundworms (phylum Nematoda), peanutworms (phylum Sipuncula), lugworms (phylum Echiura) and, most importantly in Fiordland, the segmented worms (phylum Annelida).

We'll look at each of these of these groups in turn but, as will become increasingly apparent, there are huge gaps in our knowledge. When we say our knowledge, this usually refers to the general literature. In many instances, and this is one of them, it refers to our personal lack of knowledge.

Marine flatworms undoubtedly exist in Fiordland and in large numbers, although neither of us can recall seeing one. The common name is an apt description of what these creatures look like. Externally they possess very few features with no sign of segmentation and usually very little differentiation. They are so thin that gas exchange occurs over the whole surface. Flatworms appear sluggish, gliding slowly along on a layer of secreted mucus, propelled by the beating actions of tiny hair-like cilia. Most can swim by undulating their body margins in a series of co-ordinated waves. Few marine predators will eat flatworms, presumably because this prey has a foul taste.

Most flatworms are predators, ingesting prey through their pharynx. Flatworms do not possess an anus, so all wastes are either passed through the body wall or ejected through the mouth.

We have seen ribbonworms in Fiordland. The most common, and the only species we photographed, is dark blue with a thin cream mid-dorsal line. This species, as yet unidentified, grows to around 75 millimetres. This pales into insignificance when compared with some North American ribbonworms, which reach over 30 metres.

Like the flatworms, most ribbonworms are predators. They feed through an organ called the proboscis, an apparatus which gives them their other common name of proboscis worm. The proboscis is not connected to the digestive tract and everts through a proboscis pore in front of the mouth. Some nemerteans possess a barbed proboscis. This barb or stylet repeatedly stabs its prey

(Right) **An unidentified spaghetti worm feeding amidst the colonial ascidian *Hypsistozoa fasmaria*.**

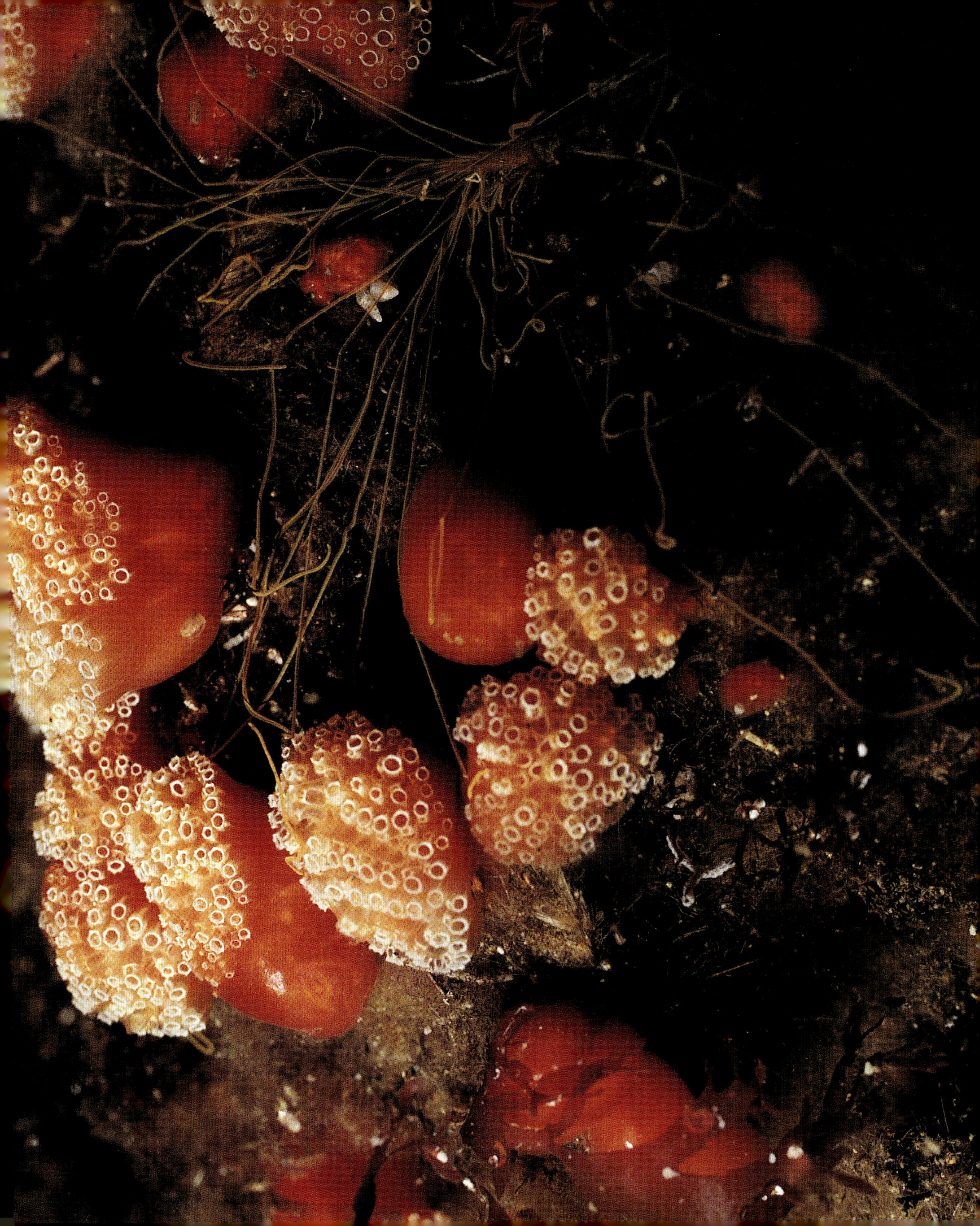

(Right) **The serpulid worm secretes a calcareous shell in which it lives. This species is** *Protula bispiralis*.

(Opposite page, Top) **Nemertean or ribbonworms are characterised by a ciliated ectoderm.**

(Opposite, Middle) **The Acorn worm** *Saccoglossus* sp. **is a detrital feeder.**

(Opposite, Lower) **A bright orange peanutworm on a sponge.**

and according to Duffy and Ackley (1988) probably pumps toxic secretions into the unfortunate victim. The proboscis coils around the prey and glandular secretions help to hold it.

Nemerteans possess several evolutionary advances over the flatworms, amongst which is the possession of an anus. This may not seem a particularly glamorous acquisition but it does allow them to continually ingest food while voiding unwanted material at the other end.

Nematodes are one of the commonest organisms on the planet. One sage claims that if the physical structure of every living thing was removed (with the exception of nematodes) a ghostly outline of their former presence would be maintained by their parasitic hordes. One species of nematode has been found in Bavarian beer mats, and to date, has yet to be discovered anywhere else. This has absolutely nothing to do with Fiordland but indicates that while the nematode fauna is not well known, it must be there in incredible numbers and diversity.

It follows from the above that almost every species in Fiordland possesses a unique nematode parasite. However, there are a number of free-living species. Typically these are less than 2.5 millimetres in length and hence difficult to see with the naked eye. Certainly there will be high numbers of nematodes in all the sandy or muddy bottoms. These species may occur at densities in the millions per square metre. These interstitial species generally feed on bacteria and adhering organic matter.

Peanutworms are small, normally insignificant creatures which appear to have evolved primarily to frustrate the memories of zoology students whose lecturers enjoy torturing them over such trivia as the name of the front section (the introvert). The introvert bears a terminal mouth and a variety of feeding structures including lobes and tentacles. These grooved and ciliated organs collect food and pass it back, conveyor belt style, to the mouth. Once the animal is full, the introvert then introverts back into the anterior end of the trunk.

Bright orange peanutworms can sometimes be seen on the surface of sponges with their introverts everted.

Lugworms have been included because they are undoubtedly common in the soft fiord bottoms. Like the peanutworms, they are usually deposit feeders. The body consists of a sausage-shaped trunk and an anterior proboscis which cannot be retracted into the trunk.

Of the segmented worms only the leeches (Hirudinea) and the bristleworms (Polychaeta) are well represented in the sea. The leeches are seldom seen, except on the occasional fish and will not be discussed further. The polychaetes however are a major contributor to the Fiordland ecosystems. Polychaetes come in a wide variety of shapes and sizes. Most commonly encountered in Fiordland are the serpulid and sabellid polychaetes.

Serpulids secrete calcareous shells in which they live. Normally they extrude their gills which act both as respiratory and feeding organs. The gills are finely divided and provide a large surface area on which tiny organic particles become trapped. They also ensure efficient gas exchange. Most tubeworms are highly sensitive to vibration and shadow. Passing a hand over the worm will almost certainly cause it to retract into the safety of its tube, while knocking the rock on which it lives will have the same effect. *Protula bispiralis* is characterised by its 'calcareous tube' and large white feeding spirals (gills).

In Fiordland, polychaetes often dominate the zone from 12 to 15 metres and make a substantial contribution to the biomass of the 7 to 12-metre zone (Grange *et al.* 1981). *Pomatoceros caeruleus* with blue/purple feeding spirals is common in the latter zone where it is subject to predation by the starfish *Sclerasterias mollis* (Grange *et al.* 1981). At greater depths serpulid polychaetes dominate. *Pomatoceros terranovae* is easily identified by its ridged tube and the bright orange feeding spirals.

Wherever there is a sandy substrate, another as yet unidentified (by the authors, but not necessarily by science) sabellid can be found. This large 'feather duster' worm *Sabella* sp. is often 75 millimetres across the gills.

Also regularly encountered are a number of reterebellid polychaetes. These fascinating creatures live in cracks, where their soft bodies are protected, and send ciliated tentacles out in search of food. These may radiate for several metres in all directions garnering organic matter from the substrate. The cilia act as a mini-conveyor belt and transport food back to the waiting mouth, where it is scooped in by a pair of palps.

The aberrant myzostomes are discussed further in the echinoderm chapter, although as far as we know, to date nobody has worked on any New Zealand species.

Free-swimming polychaetes are regularly seen during night dives. These are possibly the reproductive hind ends of polychaetes, not whole worms. One of the major problems with nocturnal underwater photography is the swarms of crustaceans and polychaetes which immediately 'mob' the torch beam. In favourable areas (to the polychaetes, not the photographer), it is difficult to take satisfactory photographs because of the density of this annelid soup.

(Left) **The tubeworm's elongate calcareous tube enables its gills to extend into the water column.**

(Opposite, Centre) **Any shadow passing over a tubeworm will cause it to immediately retract the feeding tentacles into the calcareous tube.**

(Opposite, Lower) **Terebellid worms are detrital deposit feeders.**

(Right) **The spaghetti worm's feeding tentacles gather food particles from the surrounding area.**

(Below) **The eunicid brittleworm** *Eulalia microphylla* **sp., lives in tight crevices of rocks in the intertidal.**

(Opposite page, Top Left) **The calcareous tube secreted by tubeworms forms a suitable substrate for encrusting organisms.**

(Opposite, Top Right) **In the feather duster worm** *Sabella* **sp., the extended gills act both as respiratory and feeding organs.**

(Opposite, Lower Left) **This unidentified tubeworm, often incorrectly identified in New Zealand as** *Pomatoceros terranovae,* **is a tube-dwelling species which may form large colonies but within the fiords is usually seen only in small groups.**

(Opposite, Lower Right) **The fine feeding tentacles of the terebellid worm can extend some distance away from the home tube.**

WORMS 67

7

Brachiopods

THERE was a time when brachiopods dominated the sea. They started their long dynasty some 600 million years ago and reached their peak in terms of both species and abundance during the Palaeozoic era. More than 3000 genera and tens of thousands of species are known from the fossil record, but only around 300 genera survive today.

They suffered badly at the hands of the greatest mass extinction the planet has ever known, the Permian extinction, which occurred about 250 million years ago. While dinosaurs and the Mesozoic extinctions attract the most popular attention, the Permian extinction was far greater. Only one out of every 10 species survived the end of the Permian.

Why did it happen? Palaeontologists continue to debate this, but climate change and a lowering of the sea level, perhaps partly caused by the locations of the continents at the time, may have been responsible. For the only time in the earth's history (as far as we know), all of the continents were fused into the supercontinent known as Pangea. This decreased the area of continental shelf by a huge factor and sea level drops associated with the glaciations which occurred at the time spelt doom for many coastal species.

Only a few brachiopods survived into the Mesozoic and when the continents spread apart and the ice caps melted they found that a bunch of upstarts, the bivalve molluscs, had already filled many of the available niches. The end result is that brachiopods now inhabit mainly marginal habitats. Fiordland is an exception in that the fiords do not possess powerful currents, nor are they as cold as other brachiopod habitats. If you want to see live brachiopods under relatively benign conditions, Fiordland is probably the best place on the planet.

Superficially, brachiopods look like the bivalve molluscs which displaced them so thoroughly, but the resemblance ends at the shell. Bivalve shells open and close laterally, whereas brachiopod valves close dorsally and ventrally. Typically, the ventral shell is larger than the dorsal. In some groups, the apex of the dorsal valve contains a hole rather reminiscent of a Roman lamp, hence the common name of lamp shell.

Internally, brachiopods bear no resemblance to molluscs. The interior of the animal is dominated by the lophophore. This is basically a crown of tentacles

(Right) **Neothyris lenticularis is found below 23m and appears to be free-living but attaches to small stones as a juvenile.**

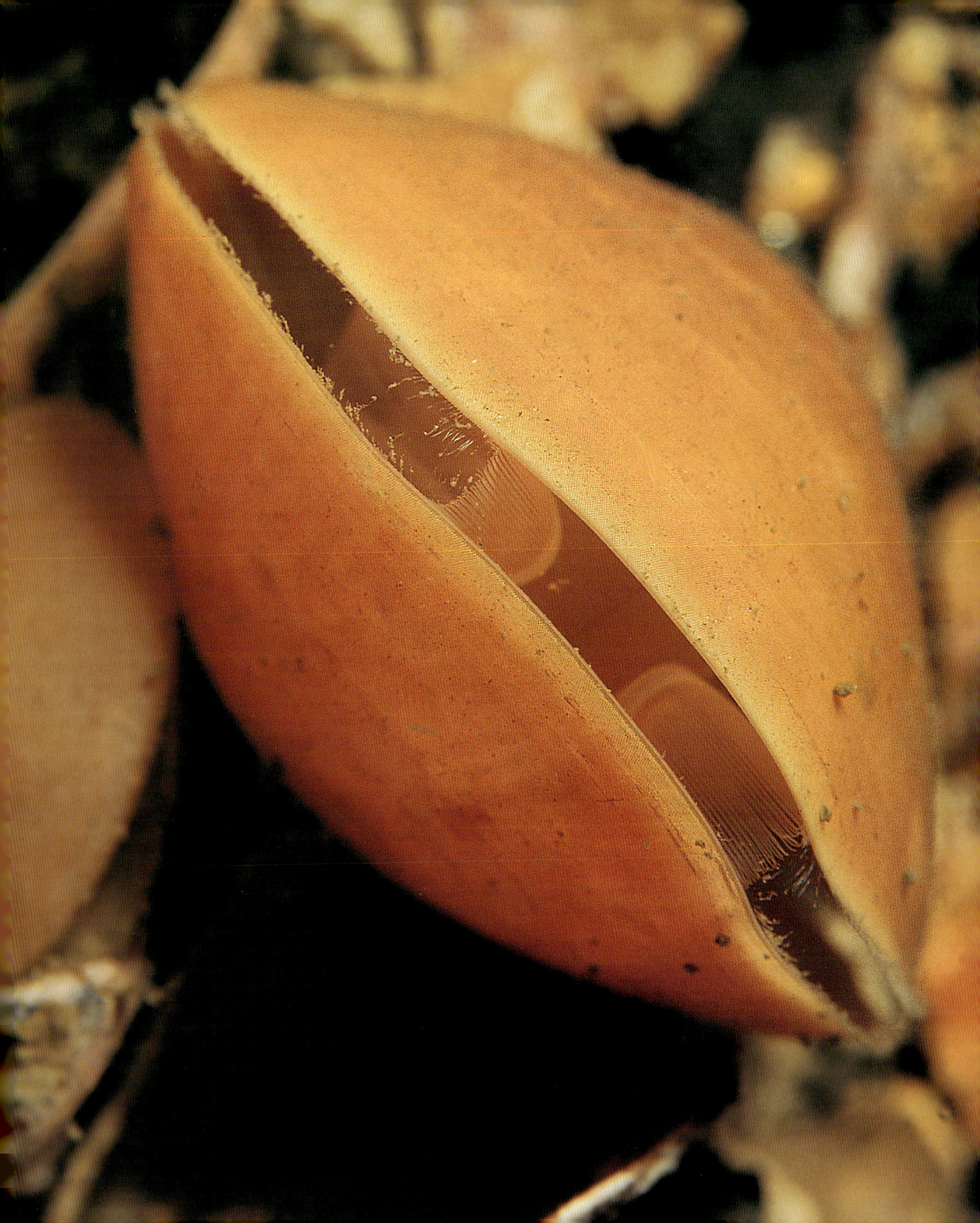

surrounding the mouth. Cilia on the tentacles pump water into the lophophore where the tentacles remove food particles. Rejected material is removed by the outflowing current.

Biologists divide the lamp shells into two clearly defined groups, the articulate and inarticulate brachiopods. The articulate brachiopods have articulated valves whereas in the inarticulates the two valves are joined only by muscles. So far most of the lamp shells identified in Fiordland belong to the articulate group, although a few inarticulate species have been dredged from the depths.

There are many places in Fiordland where brachiopods dominate large areas of the cliff-face. If you approach cautiously and shine a torch between the valves, you should be able to see the lophophore. Lamp shells attach to the wall with their pedicle, an extraordinarily strong proteinaceous thread. If this cord breaks, the brachiopod drifts into the depths and dies. It is fastened to the wall with a cement, secreted by the animal. According to Ward (1992), this cement is so strong that "it makes our synthetic cements seem ludicrous in comparison". This has inspired considerable research interest into the humble brachiopod.

Apart from their valves, lamp shells appear to have few defences. Appearances can be deceiving, as Ward describes in his book *On Methuselah's Trail*:

> My friend holds up the remains of the now thoroughly destroyed brachiopod and has derisive things to say about how little flesh there is for so large a shell. "No wonder they are almost extinct," he mumbles, and then asks me if they are any good to eat. "Don't do it!" I tell him. My friend assures me that anything taken from Puget Sounds waters is edible. "Don't do it!" I shout. He gives me his best stage sneer, the one reserved for scientists, and intones his favorite condemnation of scientists and their practical ignorance. "Too much college and not

(Left and Lower) **The scarlet *Magasella sanguinea* is the commonest and most wide-ranging brachiopod in the fiords.**

(Opposite page, Top) **The black brachiopod *Notosaria nigricans* (20 mm) has highly fluted black valves. Brachiopods abound on the rock walls of the fiords.**

(Opposite, Lower) **White brachiopod *Liothyrella neozelandea*. Brachiopods are only superficially similar to molluscs and feed by filtering seawater through a structure known as a lophopore.**

enough high school." The brachiopod, remnant of one of the great stocks of life, survivor since the earliest Palaeozoic, disappears into his mouth and plays its part in the ongoing process of evolution. Its death surely serves some purpose, for it greatly diminishes the probability that at least one human being will ever again try to eat a brachiopod: even before the wretched creature is halfway down, my friend turns green, and retches violently on the beach. I can't help myself; I roar with laughter. "One thing about college," I tell him when he regains his composure and control of his stomach, "At least they teach you not to eat brachiopods."

Should you be tempted to try, you have five common species in Fiordland to choose from. The bright scarlet *Magasella sanguinea* is the most wide-ranging and probably the most common of the lamp shells. According to Singleton (in Grange, 1990) it occurs at all depths between 5 to 35 metres with maximum abundance at 20 to 30 metres. The smallest (20 millimetres) is *Notosaria nigricans*. As the scientific name suggests, it has black valves. These are highly fluted and quite distinctive. It reaches peak abundance between 15 and 25 metres. Singleton did not record it below 30 metres. The red *Calloria inconspicua*, which is often covered by encrusting organisms, was most abundant at 10 metres and did not extend beyond 25 metres. *Waltonia* has smooth valves and grows to 20 millimetres.

The largest of our brachiopods is *Neothyris lenticularis* which grows to 50 millimetres. It is mainly found at 23 metres or deeper. Unlike the species above, it is found lying loose on sediment, but actually *Neothyris* only appears to be free-living in the adult. The pedicle of the young brachiopod is attached to a small stone or shell fragment. So far it has only been reported from Preservation Inlet. *Neothyris* comes in a range of colours including pink, grey or peach. *Liothyrella neozelandea* is also found within sport diving depths. Grange (1990) reports that it is known from shallow depths in the southern fiords, but gets deeper further north. Doubtful Sound is the most northern diving record, where it is common at depths of 20 metres.

Two other brachiopods are also recorded, *Crania huttoni* and *Amphithyris richardsonae*, but both species are rare.

Grange (1990) reports that brachiopod densities often exceed 200 per square metre in Doubtful Sound. We have seen densities far in excess of this, with rough estimates of 1000-plus per square metre.

(Left and Lower) **White brachiopod *Liothyrella neozelandea*.** Brachiopods are only superficially similar to molluscs and feed by filtering seawater through a structure known as a lophopore.

(Opposite page) **The black brachiopod *Notosaria nigricans* (20 mm)** displays highly fluted black valves.

8

Molluscs

MOST people are well acquainted with molluscs through finding the shells from the dead animals washed up on beaches. Molluscs, whose name means 'soft-bodied', secrete the hard calcareous shell using a mantle. This is a sheet of thin tissue which covers the body organs. The shell itself usually consists of one piece, although in the bivalves there are two pieces or valves, and chitons have eight separate plates.

In some sea-slugs (nudibranchs) and squid, the shell is reduced and enclosed by the body, while in other nudibranchs and octopuses it is lacking altogether. About 2000 species of molluscs have been recorded from New Zealand, but many hundreds of new species remain to be described, and others are being discovered almost on a daily basis.

Apart from the ubiquitous bivalve mussels, the most commonly seen molluscs in Fiordland are the gastropods. Most possess a single spirally coiled shell but in some this may be cap-shaped (limpets) or greatly reduced or lacking, as in the shield shell *Scutus breviculus*. All gastropods have an obvious head, usually with eyes and tentacles, and a muscular foot with which they move. The mantle encloses a cavity containing the gills. Usually the animal is able to withdraw completely into its shell, and in most coiled species, the entrance is blocked by a horny or calcareous operculum (cat's eye). Most gastropods feed by means of a radula, a tooth-bearing organ that is used to scrape algae off the substrate, for tearing flesh, for harpooning prey or for boring into shells of prey organisms.

Bivalves are also common and may be found living permanently attached to the rock walls by strong byssal threads (i.e. mussels) or unattached, partially or fully buried in sand and shell grit on ledges (i.e. scallops). As the name suggests, the shell is in two halves, and is hinged. Bivalves lack a head, although some, such as the scallop, have many eyes at the mantle edge. Most are filter feeders, taking food particles in through the inhalant siphon. Food particles are strained off in the gills and directed to the mouth. Wastes and water are ejected through the exhalant siphon.

The ecology of the molluscan fauna of Fiordland has not been studied in detail and although several hundred species of large 'macro' molluscs have been recorded and

(Right) Chitons (Amphineura) are distinctive molluscs with a flexible shell of eight interlocking plates surrounded by a tough leathery girdle, and a limpet-like foot that enables them to cling to uneven rock surfaces.

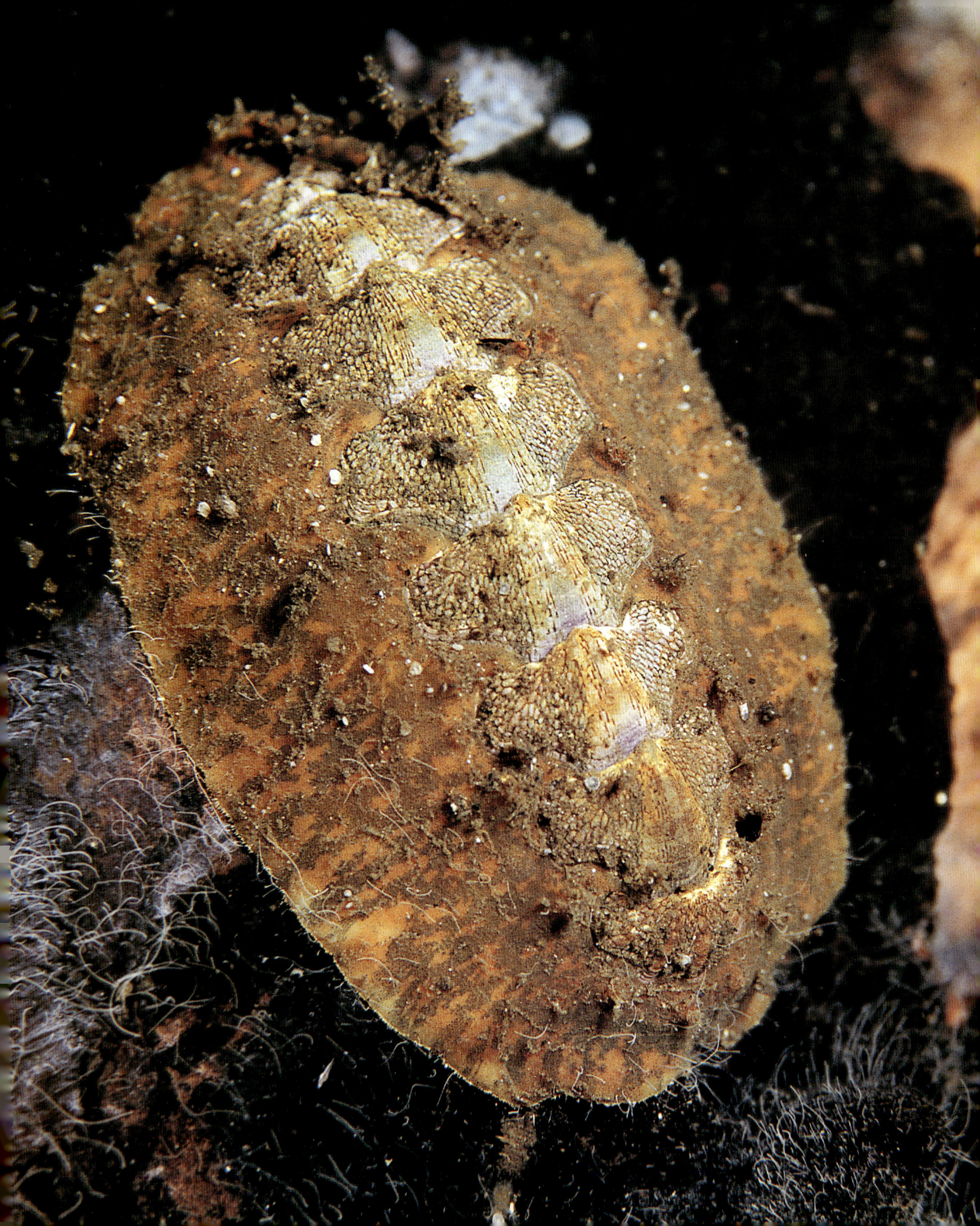

described, ongoing studies of molluscs by Bruce Marshall (Museum of New Zealand), have revealed dozens of new records, mostly in the small size range (less than 5 millimetres). These small molluscs, which constitute the greatest number of mollusc species, are often almost invisible in the algae or sand and shell grit sediments. They can be collected by washing algae over a fine sieve, or are separated from sediments by flotation on high density liquids. There are eight classes of molluscs and five of these have been recorded from Fiordland.

On the rock walls in most of the fiords there is a characteristic band of mussels, comprising the brackish water mussel *Xenostrobus securis*, the ribbed mussel *Aulacomya atramaoriana*, and the blue-lipped mussel *Mytilus galloprovincialis*. They form a thick two metre-deep band below the freshwater interface in association with green sea lettuce *Ulva* spp., and red seaweed *Rhodymenia leptophylla* (which occur only near the surface because of the poor light penetration), and barnacle *Elminius modestus*. The large predatory starfish *Coscinasterias calamaria*, can be found in large numbers below this band, moving up to prey on the mussels when the retreating freshwater layer permits.

Research by Jon Witman and Ken Grange has shown how important the freshwater layer is as a refuge from predation. They found that at 2.5 metres depth, no transplanted mussels were consumed, but below that 20 to 80 percent of the mussels were consumed, mostly by the sea-stars *C. calamaria* and *Patiriella regularis* and the urchin *Evechinus chloroticus* at five metres, and crayfish *Jasus edwardsii* at 10 metres.

Below the mussel band, in depths of 7 to 14 metres, are areas where the rock walls are less steep, shell grit and gravel accumulate and the bivalve *Ruditapes largillierti* and the turret shell *Maoricolpus roseus* are relatively common. Towards the lower depths of this zone, the scallop *Pecten novaezelandiae* and the horse mussel *Atrina zelandica* are also found. The horse mussels reach exceptional size: shell length may exceed 600 millimetres.

(Left) ***Jason mirabilis***, one of New Zealand's more spectacular sea-slugs, feeds on sea anemones and is capable of consuming undischarged anemone stinging cells, which it stores in the projections on its back for its own defence.

(Below) The warty sea-slug ***Archidoris wellingtonensis***, grazes on sponges and may reach 300 mm in Fiordland. It occurs throughout New Zealand.

(Opposite page, Top) ***Atagema carinata***, a nudibranch or sea-slug that is rare in New Zealand.

(Opposite, Middle) ***Chromodoris aureomarginata***, so named for the yellow or gold margin, grows to 60 mm and occurs off North, South and Stewart Islands.

(Opposite, Lower) ***Aphelodoris luctuosa***. Sea-slugs or nudibranchs are more common in the middle and outer fiords.

(Above) **Blue mussels** *Mytilus galloprovincialis*, attach to the rocks by a hairy byssus.

(Right) **The horse mussel** *Atrina zelandica*, reaches 600 mm in length in Fiordland, where it lives on sandy ledges throughout the fiords.

(Opposite page, Top) **Ribbed mussels** *Aulacomya atra maoriana*, form a dense band together with blue mussels below the intertidal zone.

(Opposite, Middle) **The distinctive butterfly chiton** *Cryptoconchus porosus* has the eight shelly plates almost completely covered by the greatly enlarged girdle.

(Opposite, Lower) **Chitons** are common on the outer fiord coast. More than 60 species have been recorded in New Zealand.

78 FIORDLAND UNDERWATER

On the steeper rock walls throughout this zone is a mobile epifauna of gastropods such as the cat's eye *Turbo smaragdus*, southern cat's eye *Modelia granosa*, topshell *Diloma zelandica*, Grant's maurea *Calliostoma granti*, tiger shell *Calliostoma tigris*, black turret shell *Zeacumantus subcarinatus*, virgin paua *Haliotis virginea*, butterfly chitons *Cryptoconchus porosus* and green chiton *Amaurochiton glaucus*.

From below 14 to 20 metres to about 40 metres depth the turban shell *Cookia sulcata*, circular saw shell *Astraea heliotropium*, trumpet shell *Charonia lampas*, swollen trumpet shell *Argobuccinum pustulosum tumidum*, sessile grooved fan shell *Mesopeplum convexum*, fan shell *Talochlamys gemmulata* and green false oyster *Pododesmus zelandicus* are found, decreasing in abundance with depth. Freshwater lowers the salinity at river deltas near the heads of the fiords and they are dominated by the cockle *Austrovenus stutchburyi*, and the pipi *Paphies australis*. In rocky areas a species of chiton and the brackish water snail *Potamopyrgus estuarinus* dominate.

Paua *Haliotis iris* form the basis of an important commercial fishery, particularly on the outer coast and near the fiord entrances. Paua are particularly abundant at these exposed localities; however, studies by Paul McShane (NIWA) have revealed that there was a complete absence of juvenile shellfish, although they were present in more sheltered areas of the fiords. Immigration of juvenile paua to the exposed coasts rather than transport of planktonic larvae is responsible for maintaining the populations. There is accumulating evidence that stocks of paua are being depleted.

The large (100 to 120 millimetres long) shield shell *Scutus breviculus* is occasionally seen under overhangs just below the red and brown algal band, where it feeds at night. The shield shell is related to the paua, but has a much reduced shell that covers only the centre of the back of the animal, and is more or less obscured by thin folds of black skin so that the animal resembles a shell-

(Top left) **The tiger shell *Calliostoma tigris*,** grows up to 100 mm in height, and is not only the largest species of Maurea top shell found in New Zealand, but the largest in the world.

(Top Right) ***Maoricolpus roseus*** **(86 mm)** is a common turret shell in the sheltered waters of Fiordland.

(Mid Left) **Grant's Maurea *Calliostoma granti*,** occurs subtidally. Like the tiger shell, it is a carnivore and feeds mainly on hydroids.

(Mid Right) **Cook's turban shell *Cookia sulcata* (115 mm).**

(Lower Left) **Whelks such as *Argobuccinum pustulosum tumidum* are unobtrusive but found throughout the fiords.**

(Lower Right) **The circular saw shell *Astraea heliotropium* (122 mm).**

(Opposite page) **The whelk *Cominella nassoides haroldi* attains 40 mm in length.**

80 FIORDLAND UNDERWATER

less paua. Also in this zone are numbers of turban shell *Cookia sulcata*, and green topshell *Trochus viridis*. Smaller specimens are found grazing on brown algae fronds, and they move to coralline paint as they grow larger.

Nudibranchs (sea-slugs) are not particularly common in Fiordland but are distinctive and easily recognised. The beautiful pink and white *Jason mirabilis* grows to 75 millimetres and can often be encountered in association with the hydroids on which it feeds. Other regularly seen species are the white *Atagema carinata* and the large *Archidoris wellingtonensis*, which can often be seen during the day hiding in crevices on rock walls.

Small octopuses are found in the outer fiords. These fiord octopuses are distinctive, with raised papillae on the greyish-brown skin which may be mottled with reds and orange to blend with the substrate. Two ocelli (false eyes) on the dorsal surface of the mantle distinguish these small octopuses from their larger and more common cousins.

According to Steve O'Shea (NIWA) there are about 20 littoral species of 'Octopus' recognised throughout New Zealand waters; however, only two species are recognised from Fiordland, *Pinnoctopus cordiformis* (= *Octopus maorum*) and *Octopus huttoni*. *Pinnoctopus cordiformis* is the large common species found throughout New Zealand from intertidal to 600 metres depth; *Octopus huttoni* is known only from littoral depths around the southern South Island. The Fiordland specimens of *Octopus huttoni* reach the largest sizes recognised for this species. A closely related species is found in Australia.

Octopuses have benefited greatly from the introduction of canned and bottled beer and the invention of the wheel. Empty cans, bottles and tyres provide ideal refuges for these species on otherwise flat sediment plains. Fiordland fishermen soon recognised that these predators of the commercial crayfish stocks were becoming more abundant and the disposal of such rubbish into the fiords is now banned by a Code of Practice.

The molluscan fauna of the deep fiord basins is generally low in diversity, resembling the deep anoxic sulphide-rich muds of the ocean floor. These deeper waters support populations of bivalves such as *Lucinoma galatheae*, *Neilo australis* and *Pratulum pulchellum*, and tusk shells *Fissidentalium zelandicum*. Numerous shells of fan shell *Talochlamys gemmulata* and *Clyclochlamys transenna* and other shallow living species that have fallen off the fiord walls are also found here.

(Right) **Octopus huttoni** is the smaller of the two species of octopus that are known from Fiordland.

(Below) **Micro-molluscs (here seen with a match-head),** are the most abundant mollusc species but can only be seen under magnification. They live on a wide variety of habitats and are collected by washing algae over a fine sieve, or by sorting them from sand on ledges in the fiords.

(Opposite page, Top Left) **The trumpet shell** Charonia lampas **(260 mm), feeds on cushion starfish and sea-urchins.**

(Opposite, Top Right) **The spiny scallop** Talochlamys gemmulata**, which has both valves convex and can be easily distinguished from the common scallop, which has one valve flat.**

(Opposite, Middle Left) **The nocturnal sea-hare** Aplysia dactylomela.

(Opposite, Middle Right) **The silver paua** Haliotis australis **is smaller than the common paua** Haliotis iris**, that forms the basis for a commercial fishery in the outer fiords and on the open coast.**

(Opposite, Below Left) **The common scallop** Pecten novaezelandiae**, has eyes all around the mantle edge.**

(Opposite, Below Right) **The shield shell** Scutus breviculus**, resembles a shell-less paua as the reduced shell is covered by folds of skin.**

MOLLUSCS 83

9

Crustaceans

WITH the exception of crayfish *Jasus edwardsii*, you are unlikely to see many free-living crustaceans in Fiordland – most are either too small or only come out at night. Unlike other areas of New Zealand, the intertidal zone within the inner fiord is depauperate of crustaceans (except for the ubiquitous shrimp *Palaemon affinis*) because of the freshwater layer. However, towards the outer coast barnacles *Elminius modestus* form a distinct band along the rock walls and careful observation will reveal shrimps, hermit crabs and the occasional true crab. Pycnogonids are also common in areas of seaweed, particularly *Macrocystis*.

Pycnogonids, or sea spiders are not true crustaceans and are classified in a separate Class Pycnogonida. They live in all oceans, including the polar seas and range in size from 1 to 10 millimetres, but are rarely seen. Most are generally drab in coloration. The body is narrow and composed of a number of distinct segments. Each segment has two lateral processes with a leg articulating at the end of each, giving the animal the appearance of being all legs and no body. The advantage of the long jointed legs can be seen when the animal is dislodged from the weed. Immediately it folds the legs over its body, forming a structure resembling the shape of a space re-entry capsule. This enables the pycnogonid to sink rapidly, but as soon as any substrate – weed or rock – is encountered, the legs are instantly splayed out and cling.

Barnacles are crustaceans, but unlike the crabs, shrimps and crayfish, they have a sessile lifestyle: all feeding, excretion and breeding takes place through the same opening in the shell. The estuarine barnacle *Elminius modestus* is found throughout New Zealand and is common in the sheltered waters of the fiords. This species forms an extensive crust over the rocks in a distinct band. Year-round breeding enables them to invade any new area of bare rock and they are important colonisers of the frequent landslips. The shell is composed of eight interconnecting plates; four make up the shell and four comprise the lid.

Many sessile invertebrates have solved the problem of getting sperm and eggs together for fertilisation by synchronising with the phases of the moon and releasing millions of gametes into the water column at once. Barnacles however, do not do this; they are hermaphroditic and swap sperm to fertilise one another's eggs – to

(Right) **The half crab *Petrolisthes elongatus* (15 mm), is common under stones in the intertidal zone and occurs abundantly in areas of suitable habitat in Fiordland.**

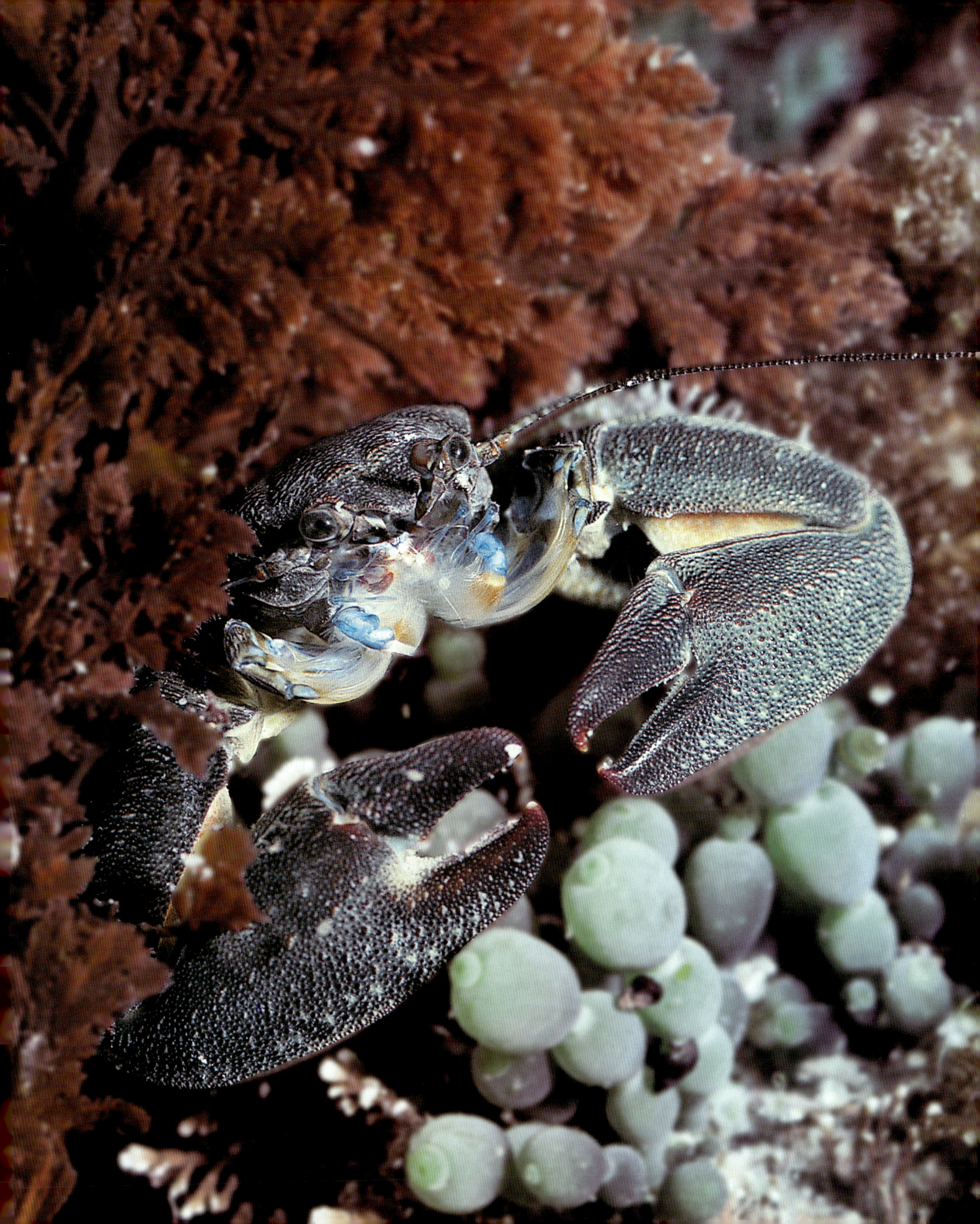

do this the male penis is extremely long in relation to the size of the body. Eggs hatch inside the protective shell of the adult and the free-swimming larvae are released to undergo several life stages until they settle onto a selected area of rock, become attached and develop into the sessile adult.

Crayfish, or rock lobster, are common throughout the fiords, and provide the basis for a multi-million dollar rock lobster fishery. Approximately one third of New Zealand's rock lobster comes from the Fiordland region. During the day they lurk in crevices and under rocks with only their long antennae showing. Because of the light-reducing freshwater layer, in some shady areas, vast numbers of crayfish may be seen on the rock walls. In these areas crayfish may be locally abundant, but the aggregations are irregular in distribution, and often associated with patches of black coral and other sessile invertebrates.

Fishermen have set pots throughout the fiords in virtually every available site; however, there are many areas too steep to place a pot, although scuba divers can easily access and see dozens of crays within a few metres. Unless careful management of this recreational fishery is introduced, the sight of large crayfish aggregations may become a thing of the past.

Perhaps because of their economic value, crayfish are coming under increasing scientific scrutiny. Alistair McDiarmid (NIWA) (1995) investigated the effect of male crayfish size on reproductive success. Crayfish reproduction is a tricky affair. Males must place sperm from vents on their rearmost walking legs near the apertures from which females extrude their eggs. As these are situated at the base of the third walking leg this requires some rather complicated manoeuvring.

Alistair originally believed that the very large male rock lobsters would have problems mating with small females weighing 10 times less. Laboratory experiments revealed that the old pros were highly effective with the full size range of reproductive females. Small males however had difficulty mating with all size ranges of reproductive females. For some of them it could have been their first time and practice, after all, does make perfect.

There is a steady migration of rock lobster around and up the Fiordland coast. As the predominant currents take the larvae south and east, movement of adults in the reverse direction may compensate for this wide spread of juveniles around the southern coast of the South Island. Tagging experiments with rock lobsters have shown some impressive long distance movements of up to 1100 kilometres. These have involved the packhorse crayfish *Jasus verreauxi* which has occasionally been found in Fiordland.

Crayfish are omnivores and scavengers. Despite their lack of any apparent weaponry, they are still competent predators, especially the larger individuals. Research by Philip James (NIWA) (1995) showed that crayfish have an innate ability to open mussels. They do this by manipulating the shell until the rounded posterior end is between their mandibles and then chewing a hole in the shell. Once the hole is big enough, the tip of the first walking leg is introduced and the posterior adductor muscle is cut. After that the cray is able to part the valves and consume the flesh. Presumably they must have some way of pulling the byssal threads (which anchor the mussel) away from the rock. If the ability to open mussels is innate, one would imagine that predation on mussels occurs fairly frequently. Indeed work by Jon Witman and Ken Grange indicates widespread predation below 10 metres.

Careful examination of the encrusting community and amongst the holdfasts of seaweeds may reveal the presence of the masking or decorator crabs, *Notomithrax* spp. and *Leptomithrax* spp. These spider crab relatives decorate themselves with a variety of biological material, especially algae and sponges, which they remove from the substrate and arrange over their carapace. The end result is brilliant camouflage which makes

(Left) **The crayfish *Jasus edwardsii* is nocturnal and during the day lives in holes and crevices inside the fiords and along the outer coast. Although known commercially as rock lobster, it lacks the massive front claws of true lobsters.**

(Below Left) **A crayfish and the tentacles of a terebellid polychaete worm. The crayfish could be allowing its carapace to be cleaned by the worm, a behaviour that has not previously been recorded.**

(Below) **Barnacles are dominant intertidal animals from the heads of the fiords to the outer coast.**

(Right) **In pycnogonids or sea spiders both gut and gonads extend into each of the legs.**

(Opposite page, Top) **The detritial feeding shrimp *Palemon affinis* (75 mm) appears almost transparent but can darken its body colour to match the surroundings by expanding special chromatophore cells.**

(Opposite, Middle) **The long-armed masking crab *Leptomithrax longimanus* is a southern species. A nocturnal feeder, it hides in algae or under rocks during the day.**

(Opposite, Lower) **Hermit crabs are abundant and in many places in Fiordland more shells appear to house hermit crabs than molluscs.**

the crabs hard to see unless they move. Large spider crabs, most notably *Jacquinotia edwardsi*, are also seen occasionally but the only specimen we have observed was at night.

Cancer novaezelandiae, a robust crab up to 75 millimetres across the carapace, is often encountered close to the open sea but its abundance wanes the further you go up the fiord. It is an opportunistic predator and scavenger. Triangle crabs *Euryolambus australis* are common in crevices and under stones.

Hermit crabs are easier to find, particularly at night which is when they appear to forage. As is the case with many of the faunal groups, little appears to be known about Fiordland's hermit crabs. One species seems to prefer circular saw shells *Astraea heliotropium* and more crabs appear to be housed in these easily recognisable shells than the molluscs themselves. Hermit crabs must change shells as they grow and do so after each moult. They are specially vulnerable at this time and unless they can find a shell of the right size and shape may well get eaten by a passing fish.

The encrusting community and the holdfast communities contain a variety of tiny amphipod and isopod species. With very few exceptions, most of these are unstudied, so we are not in a position to comment further on them. Parasitic isopods *Livoneca raynaudii* are occasionally seen on the gill covers of fish. This isopod often eats the tongue of its fish host and then lies in the cavity this creates. Here it presumably steals food from its host. As the isopod is the same approximate shape as the fish tongue, it is able to survive in the mouth of its host without too much further inconvenience (except to the host).

Shrimps and prawns are not often seen but do occur in the cliff-face fauna. We have seen what appears to be a hinge-beaked shrimp in cavities in the rock wall but so far have been unable to obtain a specimen or identify it. Presumably this species is nocturnal, as we have not seen it during the day.

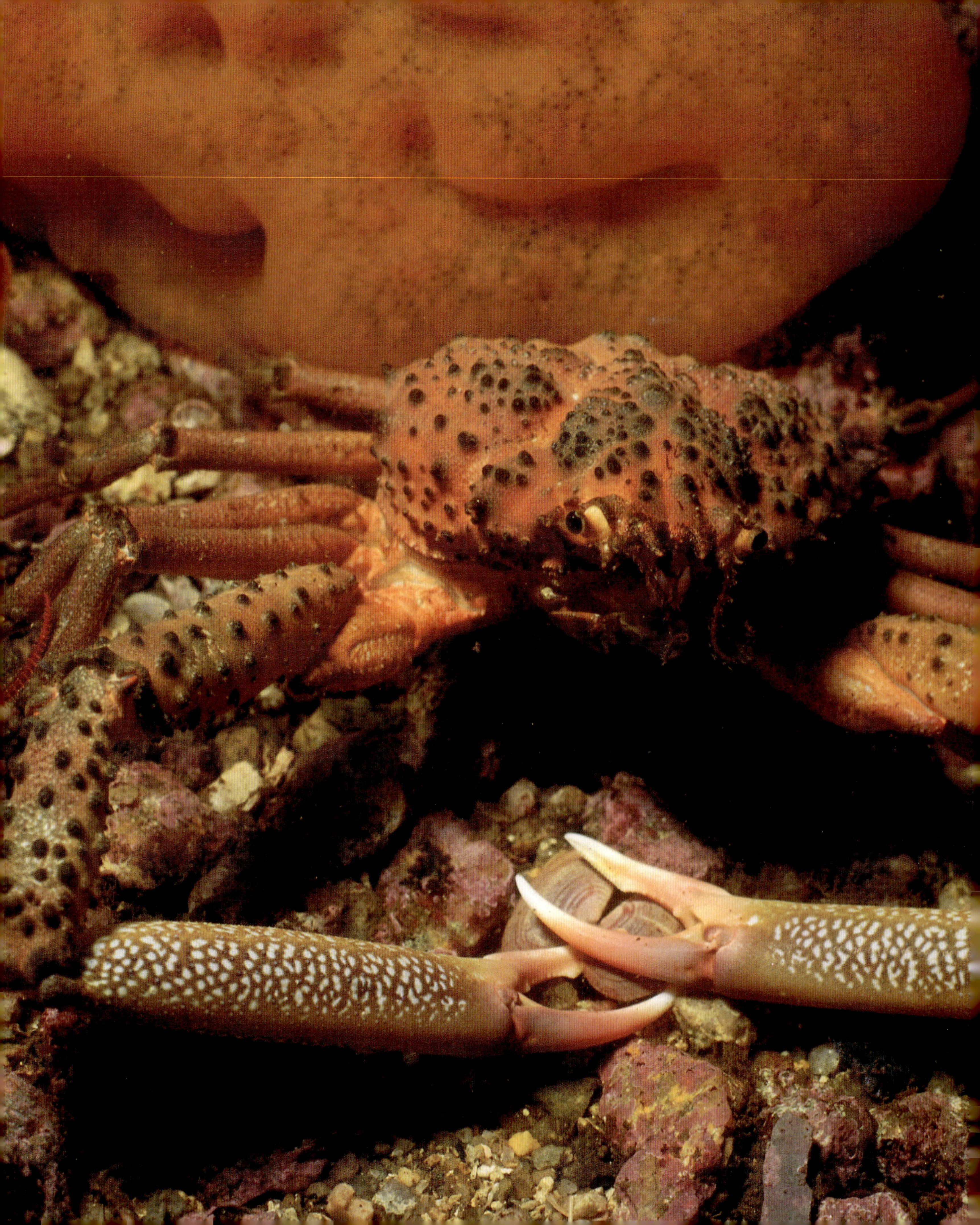

CRUSTACEANS 91

(Right) **The camouflage crab** *Notomithrax ursus* covers its carapace with available sessile organisms including seaweed and sponges.

(Below) **In the southern fiords** unidentified barnacles are common on red coral *Errina novaezelandiae*.

(Opposite page) **Hermit crabs** occupy any available shell – in this instance a rock shell *Lepsithais lacunosus*.

Previous Page:
(Left) **Long-armed masking crab** *Leptomithrax longimanus* is a southern species. During the day it hides in algae or under rocks, feeding at night.

(Right Top) **Intertidal sand flats** support populations of the tunnelling mud crab *Helice crassa* **(20 mm)**.

(Right Lower) **The nocturnal rock crab** *Cancer novaezelandiae* feeds on bivalve molluscs, which it opens by breaking the thin outer edges of the shell.

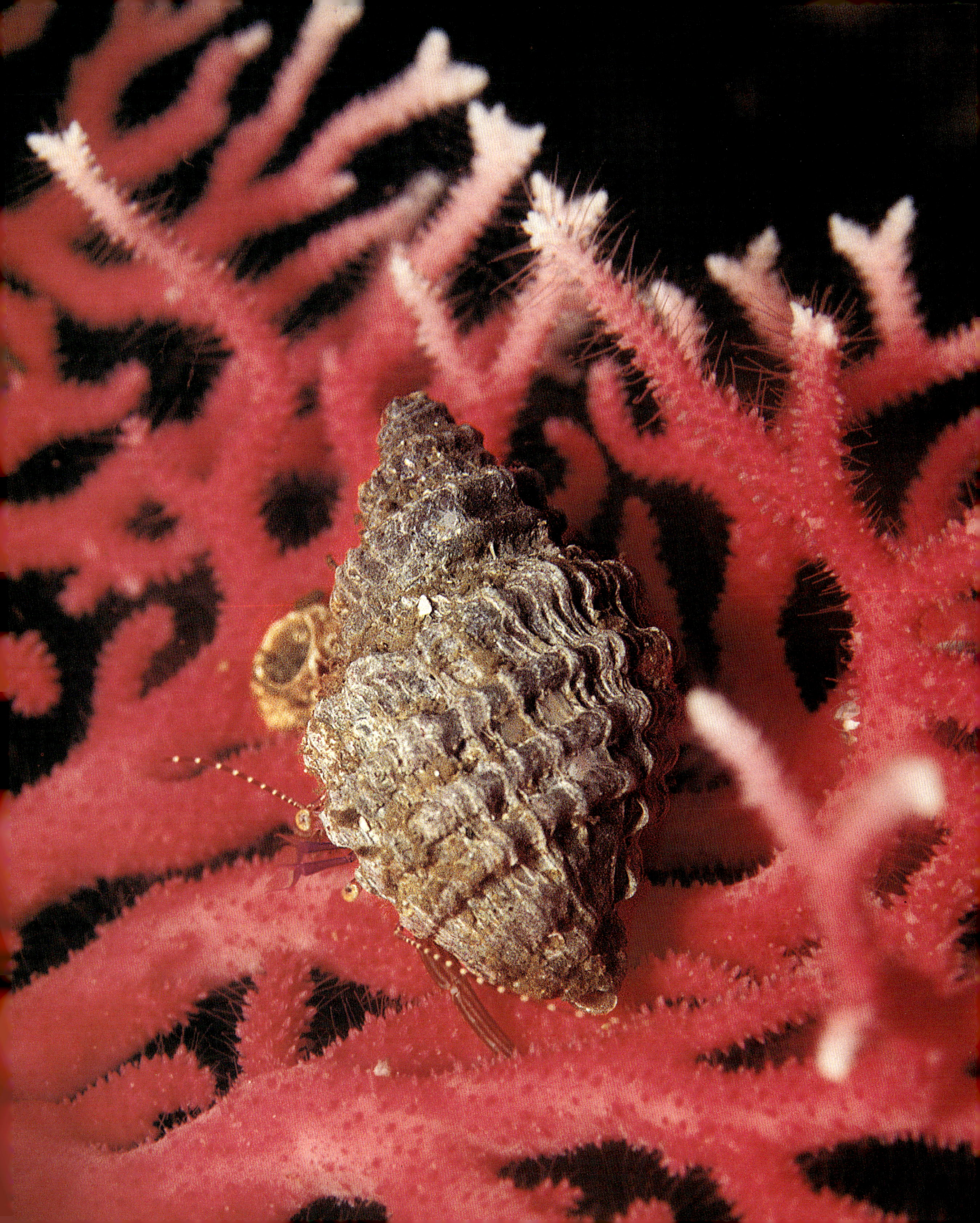

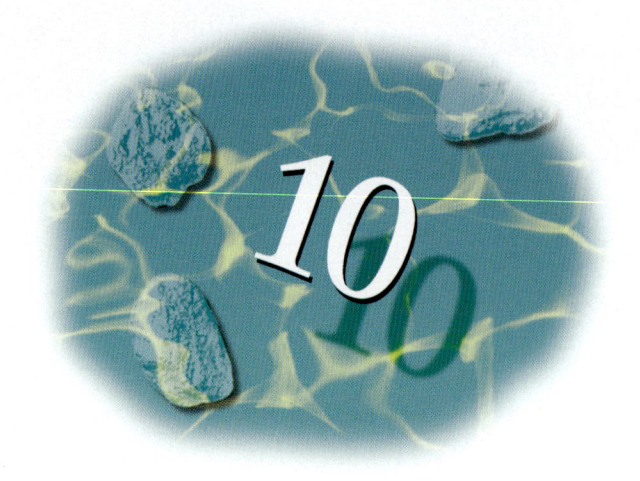

Echinoderms

ECHINODERMS constitute a rather strange phylum. Most of us recognise that they are different without actually questioning why. They provide some obvious pointers to the group. Starfish are normally depicted as five-armed even though they exhibit a gamut of formats. Unlike most other 'higher' animals, echinoderms are built on a basic five-sided symmetry rather than the bilateral symmetry we are used to. Traces of this can be seen in sea-urchins where the tube feet and spines usually occur in five bands or multiples thereof. Even the apparently bilaterally symmetrical sea-cucumbers are only secondarily bilaterally symmetrical. Their pentamerous symmetry is seen in the structure of their internal organs. Interestingly, echinoderm larvae are bilaterally structured.

With the obvious exception of sea-cucumbers, echinoderms contain a bony internal skeleton. This is covered with a thin veneer of skin. In sea-cucumbers the skeleton is reduced to a series of calcareous spicules in the skin. In most echinoderms a water vascular system, together with a series of muscles, provides hydrostatic pressure and enables a series of tube feet to propel the animal. These thin-walled appendages also enable some gas exchange ('breathing') to occur. Thin-walled sacs (papulae) extrude through the upper surface of starfish and also play a role in gas exchange.

In the starfish and sea-urchins a series of extraordinary grapnel-jawed devices keep the animal clear from settling organisms or silt. In some tropical species these pedicellariae are venomous and in the flower urchin *Toxopneustes pileolus* these can cause death in susceptible individuals. For most of us, the sharp sea-urchin spines are sufficient deterrent for us to stay away.

Four major classes make up the phylum. These are the Stelleroidea (starfish and brittlestars), Echinoidea (sea-urchins, heart urchins and sand dollars), Holothuroidea (sea-cucumbers) and the Crinoidea (the sea-lilies and featherstars).

Echinoderms are a major component of the Fiordland underwater ecology and are noticed almost immediately by anyone who scuba dives in the fiords. In terms of biomass, the echinoderms may well be the dominant creatures at diveable depths. Kina graze right into the freshwater layer while just below the mussel beds, hordes of apparently ravenous *Coscinasterias calamaria* starfish

(Right) **The eleven-arm starfish *Coscinasterias calamaria* at 6m depth, surrounded by strawberry holothurians *Ocnus* sp.**

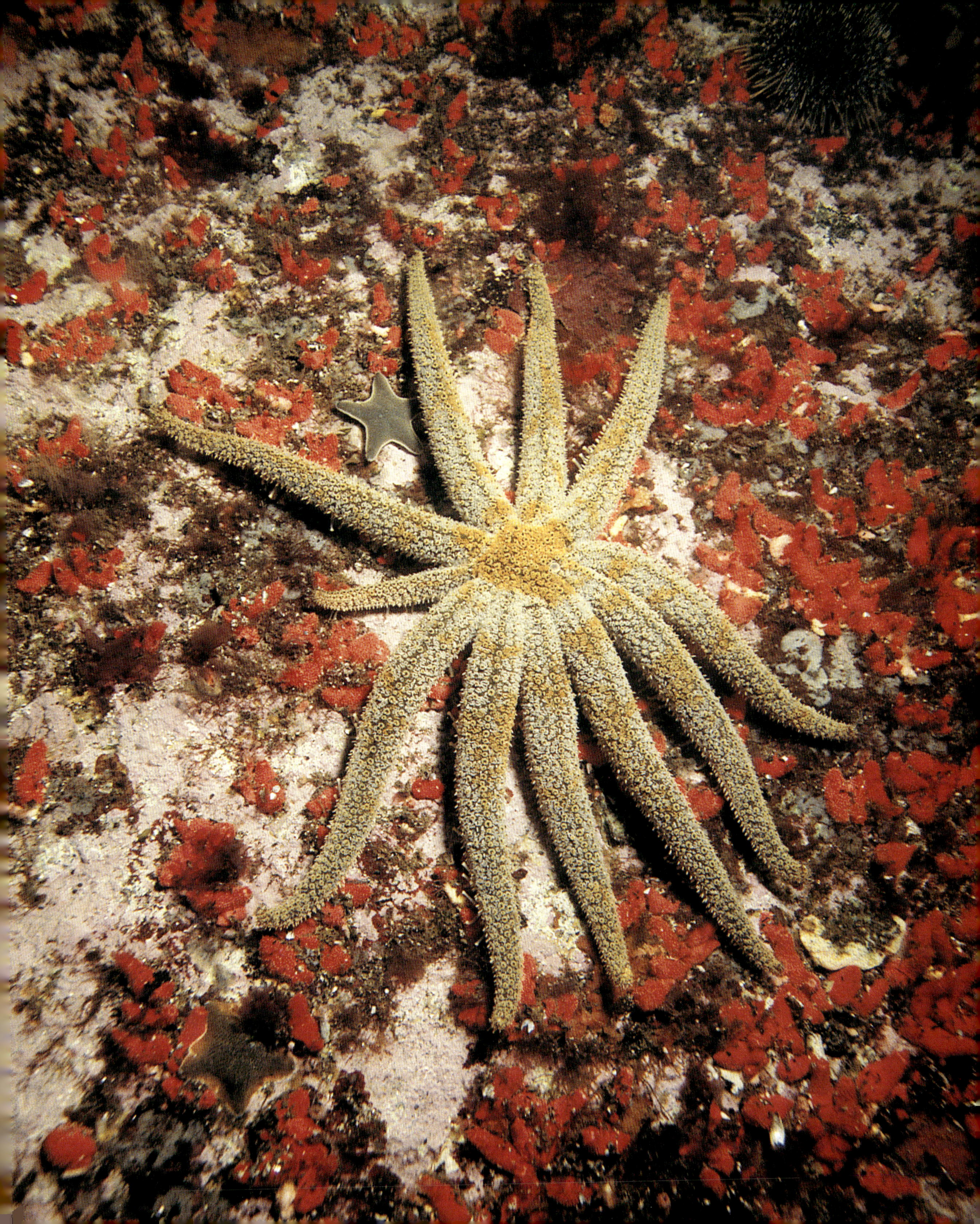

lie in wait. Snakestars cling tightly to black coral and common sea-cucumbers lie around on any flat areas, where they feed on the deposits which accumulate.

The commonest starfish in Fiordland is almost certainly the small (up to 100 millimetres) cushionstar *Patiriella regularis* which, unlike its giant relative *Coscinasterias*, is quite at home in the low salinity surface layer. The cushionstar has between four and seven arms, although five is normal. They are usually detritus feeders, everting their stomachs over suitable material and digesting it directly. However, they will take advantage of any opportunity. We have seen ravening hordes of *Patiriella* eating moribund salps. *Patiriella* range widely through the fiords and can be found at all diveable depths.

The large *Coscinasterias calamaria* is found from sea level down to 25 metres (Grange *et al.* 1981). The upper limit depends upon the thickness of the freshwater layer into which *Coscinasterias* will not venture. Under drought conditions (which, surprisingly, do occur in Fiordland) the *Coscinasterias* phalanx wreaks havoc amongst the mussel band. While variable in colour, *Coscinasterias* is usually orange, although this may not be apparent under the filtered light of the fiord. The mass congregation of this spectacular starfish under the freshwater layer is one of the highlights of any Fiordland dive.

According to Bradstock (1989) the population structure of this species varies from area to area, from equal numbers of males and females to colonies dominated five to one by females. In Otago Harbour there is an entirely male colony. This may be due to differential survival of the larvae but this does not solve the problem; it simply delays it one stage.

Once such a skewed sex ratio colony is established it tends to maintain itself by asexual reproduction. Splitting in two may follow periods of stress. The two halves of the starfish just walk in different directions. Each half then regenerates the missing arms.

The starfish *Sclerasterias mollis* is also commonly

(Left) Featherstars, *Oxycomanthus plectrophorum*, are rarely encountered elsewhere in depths as shallow as they are found in the fiords.

(Opposite page, Top) The brittlestar *Ophiomyxa brevirima*, is found under stones where it feeds on detritus.

(Opposite, Middle) Central disc of *Coscinasterias*.

(Opposite, Lower) Snakestars *Pectinura maculata* are found throughout the fiords.

(Right) **Eleven-arm starfish form a band below the freshwater layer where they wait for it to recede to gain access to the mussel zone.**

(Opposite page, Top) *Astrostole scabra* **is New Zealand's largest starfish and may reach 700 mm across.**

(Opposite, Middle) *Eurygonias hylacanthus* **belongs to a group of starfish which brood their young beneath a gelatinous membrane covering the surface.**

(Opposite, Lower) *Asteroceras elegans* **occurs only on gorgonians.**

encountered at depths down to 15 metres. It feeds mainly on the tubeworm *Potamoceros caeruleus*, the bivalve mollusc *Venerupis largillierti* and the gastropod *Maoricolpus roseus* (Grange *et al.* 1981). This orange and cream starfish is remarkably fragile. If you attempt to move one, it will shed arms or split, seemingly accidentally. However, it is capable of regeneration from the broken pieces and several new starfish will arise.

Astrostole scabra, the seven-armed starfish, may occasionally be seen. This is the largest New Zealand starfish and some specimens can reach up to 700 millimetres across the arms. The seven-armed starfish comes in a variety of colours ranging from brown, grey, blue, purple or pink or even a combination of these colours. It is a voracious carnivore which favours chitons and trochid snails (Duffy and Ackley, 1988). In our experience, it is not common in Fiordland.

Pentagonaster pulchellus, the common biscuitstar, is often seen at depths of 1 to 10 metres. While some specimens are a fiery orange elsewhere in the country, we have yet to observe this morph in Fiordland. Most specimens are brown or purple-brown. Although reasonably common, these starfish are worth a second look. The central disk is formed from a variety of delicately sculpted plates.

There are many rare asteroids found throughout the fiords. *Asterodon miliaris* is a small (75 millimetres across the arms) bright orange biscuitstar. Its intense colour immediately distinguishes it from its background. Two other orange starfish, *Henricia lukinsii* and *Allostichaster insignus*, are also infrequently encountered but occasionally locally abundant. *Allostichaster* has thicker arms than *Henricia* and is covered with a series of raised papillae. By contrast, *Henricia* is almost 'hairy' rather than 'knobby'.

The brittlestars and snakestars are well described by their common names. Generally, brittlestars lose their arms easily, while snakestars have excellent mobility in their arms. As far as biologists are concerned, there is

(Right) ***Astrobrachion constrictum*** feed at night by stealing food from the coral polyps. The coral also benefits though, as the snakestar clears sediment which could smother the colony.

(Opposite page, Top) ***Astrobrachion constrictum*** is found in a variety of colour morphs.

(Opposite, Lower) ***Astrobrachion constrictum*** remains tightly coiled during the day, possibly to avoid predators.

no real distinction between the two. This subclass is the most successful of all the echinoderms both in numbers of individuals and numbers of species. This is partly due to their presence on the sea floor in even the abyssal depths where deposits of detritus are available, albeit in small quantities.

Some brittlestars are versatile in their feeding methods, able to skim food from the water surface as the tide moves in, or by utilising deposits, or by removing particles from the water column. Because of the fresh-water layer, this is not an option for any Fiordland species.

Probably the commonest ophiuroid in Fiordland is the red and black snakestar *Pectinura maculata*. This large snakestar (up to 300 millimetres across the arms), is a predator and scavenger. During the Museum of New Zealand fish collecting trips, most of us had the experience of trying to race red and black snakestars to drugged fish. While they are common above 20 metres, they reach their maximum density below this depth and Grange *et al.* (1981) report densities of three per square metre, with the arms of adjacent individuals often touching.

The mottled sandstar *Ophionereis fasciata* is not so frequently encountered. This isn't too surprising, as the stone-covered sand environment it requires is not common in Fiordland. The mottled sandstar is a detritus feeder which gleans its food by brushing the surface with sticky secreted mucus underlying the arms. The tube feet both secrete the mucus and pass the trapped particles along the arm to the mouth.

Black coral colonies characterise Fiordland. However it is only recently that the role of snakestars in their survival has been discovered (Grange 1991). Ken Grange noticed that black coral colonies without snakestars tended to become covered in silt. Silt-covered colonies looked in considerably worse shape than those with snakestars, so he suggested that perhaps the snakestar played a part in keeping its host healthy.

The snakestar is normally the deep red, yellow or black

ECHINODERMS *101*

and white banded *Astrobrachion constrictum*. *Astrobrachion* robs food from its black coral host. In doing so it also keeps the black coral clean so it ends up being a truly mutualistic relationship. Despite the claims of various textbooks, true mutualism is relatively rare in nature. Usually one partner gets a much better deal than the other. *Astrobrachion* will also glean plankton by extending its arms into the water column. The brown and white-spotted *Astroceras elegans* has been found in Caswell Sound where it occurs only on gorgonians (Grange *et al*. 1981). We also found specimens in Preservation Inlet and Franz Smith has reported them from Doubtful Sound.

Kina *Evechinus chloroticus*, is the commonest sea-urchin at the entrances to the fiords and wherever there is substantial algal growth. Elsewhere the white or pink sea-urchin *Pseudechinus huttoni* dominates. Kina need little introduction, but their lifestyle is probably alien to most of us. Mike Bradstock (1989) admirably summarises their feeding habits in his book *Between the Tides*:

> The urchin's usual food is seaweed, fragments of which are plucked from the surge with the tube-feet like wind-blown leaves. But this adaptable animal will also graze rock surfaces, gravel, or sandy ground, grinding in its powerful jaws whatever it finds – sponges, anemones, bryozoans, detritus and fuzzy growths of micro-organisms. They are like eating machines, devouring even the moulted shells of crayfish and the slow growth of decay which covers waterlogged wooden branches jammed by surge between boulders. Since they do not always have to move to feed, it is easy to see why they can live virtually cheek-by-jowl in some places, clutching fragments of weed for future meals. The more food available the faster they grow, and the longer they seem to live.

Their voracious appetite seems to be causing problems

(Left) *Patiriella regularis* feeds voraciously on mussels but it will also scavenge any dead animals.

(Below) *Coscinasterias* brown morph. In many starfish, the animal can regenerate lost arms, and in some instances new starfish will develop from the amputated arm.

(Opposite page, Top and Lower) *Patiriella regularis* is the commonest starfish in Fiordland.

ECHINODERMS

(Right) *Evechinus* or kina is a delicacy both for Maori and Japanese; however Fiordland specimens are too bitter to eat.

(Opposite page, Top) The predatory starfish *Stegnaster inflatus*, forms an arch and immediately clamps down on any fish or shrimp that enters.

(Opposite, Lower) The brilliant *Asterodon miliaris* brightens many fiord walls.

104 FIORDLAND UNDERWATER

in parts of the New Zealand coast. Whole areas have been denuded of large algae such as *Ecklonia* by kina grazing activities. The reasons are still obscure but could be because of increased fishing pressure causing removal of kina predators. Crayfish, snapper and blue cod all fit this category. However there are areas of high kina density where their predators are also common so this simple cause-and-effect scenario is more complicated than first appears.

Kina in Fiordland were subjected to a comprehensive census in Dusky Sound to determine whether or not the animals could be harvested for their roe. After considerable effort had been expended it was discovered that roe from Fiordland kina are occasionally too bitter to eat. Yet the survey had valuable spinoffs and gained useful information about the role of kina in controlling the growth of algae and encrusting organisms. Eduardo Villouta and Chris Pugsley (DoC), together with a band of dedicated helpers, moved five tonnes of kina at various survey sites. Seaweed abundance increased markedly after kina removal, suggesting that kina play an important role in seaweed distribution.

Other recent kina work in Fiordland has been by Miles Lamare (1995). Earlier research indicated that Fiordland kina were genetically different from those in the rest of the country. Miles set out to determine if the Fiordland kina bred within the fiord system. His Doubtful Sound study revealed mass spawning in November. Vertical plankton tows at selected sites through the fiord showed that maximum densities of planula larvae occurred in mid-fiord. Few larvae were captured beyond the sill at the entrance. This suggests that the Fiordland kina are genetically isolated from populations elsewhere. This work has profound implications for the genetic character of each fiord. Not only may they be isolated from the rest of the country but they may be isolated from each other.

The dominant urchin of the walls and fallen trees is the white or pink *Pseudechinus huttoni*. This urchin appears to eat anything. Fallen trees are soon attacked by this animal but we don't know whether it is actively digesting the wood or encrusting organisms which have settled on the tree. Kina characteristically cover themselves with bits of algae which they then eat at their leisure. The white urchin covers itself with beech and other forest leaves. Again it is not known whether this is for a food supply or to camouflage the animal. The food supply scenario seems the most likely as the urchins are rarely well enough covered for camouflage to be a real option. Peter Johnson of Landcare Otago points out that some of the landslides in Fiordland range from the sub-alpine zone right down to sea level. We thus have the extraordinary spectacle of sea-urchins munching their way through sub-alpine plants carried into the water by the slip. The phenomenon is unlikely to be seen anywhere else in the world.

Occasionally orange urchins *Pseudechinus albocincta* are encountered.

Hurley (1964) found the heart urchin *Echinocardium cordatum* dominated the soft bottom community of the inner basin. Ken Grange *et al.* (1981) also encountered this species on sandy bottoms in Preservation Inlet at depths of 25 to 30 metres. Heart urchins spend most of their life burrowing, so may not be evident even if they are present. They feed on organic material in the sand.

Only one species of sea-cucumber is widespread in Fiordland. *Stichopus mollis*, the same species found throughout New Zealand, lives here in reasonable numbers. In fact proposals have been made to harvest *Stichopus* for subsequent treatment and export to South East Asia as trepang (the dried and smoked body of the sea-cucumber minus its internal organs). In the 1980s exploratory fishing was undertaken. Properly controlled, such a scheme could be sustainable but with the high Fiordland rainfalls the necessary air-drying of the catch proved to be impractical.

Stichopus come in a variety of colours and body shapes. Some are covered in quite marked protuberances while others are nearly smooth. This sea-cucumber reaches 200 millimetres. If it is severely threatened, *Stichopus*, in common with many other holothurians, will expel its internal organs through its anus.

Common on cliff-faces but small and easily overlooked is *Ocnus brevidentis*. This small white sea-cucumber extends elegant feeding tentacles into the water column and traps suspended particles. If you find one of these and can get close enough without disturbing it you will see the tentacles deposit material into the mouth. Any incautious move though will cause the tentacles to retract.

Much brighter, but found in only a few isolated localities is the strawberry sea-cucumber *Ocnus* sp. This spectacular scarlet holothurian grows to around 75 millimetres. In the one place we've visited where this animal is found, it dominates the zone just below the freshwater layer. On close examination most strawberry sea-cucumbers carry tiny gastropod molluscs. These are parasitic and have previously been reported only from depths of around 1000 metres. Although small (5 to 10 millimetres), they are easily seen because the animal glows with an eerie lime-yellow bioluminescence. The strawberry sea-cucumber is also normally a deep water species but in Fiordland joins the emergent fauna that makes the place so special. Our locality was discovered by Lance Shaw and named 'Strawberry Fields'. Disturbed strawberry sea-cucumbers contract until they look indistinguishable from strawberries. They were only at eight metres, so we weren't suffering from nitrogen narcosis when we made this observation.

Several tiny holothurians can be seen amongst the complex cliff-face communities, but to date we have neither photographs nor identifications.

Featherstars are characterised by their highly divided pinnate arms, a tiny central disc and a series of cirri which hold them to their perch. They filter small organisms and organic matter from the water using the small branches or pinnules. These give the arms a feathery appearance and hence their common name. Trapped food particles are carried to the mouth by the beating of cilia contained within a groove in the centre of each arm.

Starfish are found in a spectacular variety of colours in Fiordland waters. Underwater, they appear dull, as longer wavelengths of light are filtered out, but a dive torch or camera flash reveals their intensity.

(Clockwise from Top Left) *Asterodon* sp.; *Henricia* sp.; *Henricia* sp.; *Stichaster* sp.; *Apteraster* sp.; *Pentagonaster pulchellus*. The common biscuitstar *Pentagonaster pulchellus* is often seen at depths of 1 to 10m throughout the fiords.

ECHINODERMS

Featherstars are commonly seen in Fiordland. They are particularly noticeable in the middle fiords where they can be seen perched on dead black coral trees or rocks. Grange (1990) notes that *Oxycomanthus plectrophorum* is found in the zone 6 to 30 metres and is rarely encountered at such shallow depths elsewhere in its range.

In the tropics, featherstars host a variety of parasites and freeloaders. These include fish, shrimps, isopods, amphipods, galatheid crabs, gastropod molluscs and a variety of worms including the extraordinary myzostomes, aberrant polychaetes. These tiny disc-shaped worms glide over the featherstar like miniature frisbees. Whether they commonly infest our featherstars is yet another of Fiordland's unknowns. This extraordinary menagerie is probably a reflection of the great antiquity of featherstars as a group which has allowed the co-evolution of so many freeloaders (most steal food; others eat podia, water-filled tubes which push food onto the ciliary conveyor belt which takes food to the mouth).

So far sea-lilies have not been reported from diveable depths in Fiordland. However, in the early 1990s a new crinoid representing a new Order for New Zealand was discovered, but to date has not been formally recorded.

While not the most glamorous of organisms, the echinoderms are the dominant mobile invertebrate fauna in Fiordland. Further research in Fiordland will undoubtedly reveal many new species and it may yet prove possible to harvest kina or sea-cucumbers on a sustainable basis, if various fundamental problems can be resolved.

(Left) *Allostichaster insignis*, an uncommon starfish in Fiordland.

(Opposite Top and Middle) *Henricia* spp. The rough appearance of the starfish surface is due to spines as well as cleaning and protective devices called pedicellariae.

(Opposite Lower) The snake-star *Pectinura maculata* is remarkably mobile and will quickly engulf a dead fish. It is also acutely light-sensitive and rapidly hides when a light is shone on it.

(Right) **These strawberry holothurians, *Ocnus* sp., are unique amongst New Zealand sea-cucumbers because of their intense coloration.**

(Opposite page, Top Left) **Feeding tentacles of the white sea-cucumber *Ocnus brevidentis*. These filter organic material from the water column.**

(Opposite, Top Right) **The white sea-urchin *Pseudechinus huttoni* is the dominant urchin below 10m, where it feeds on decaying organic material.**

(Opposite, Lower) ***Stichopus mollis*, the sea-cucumber, is widespread throughout the fiords.**

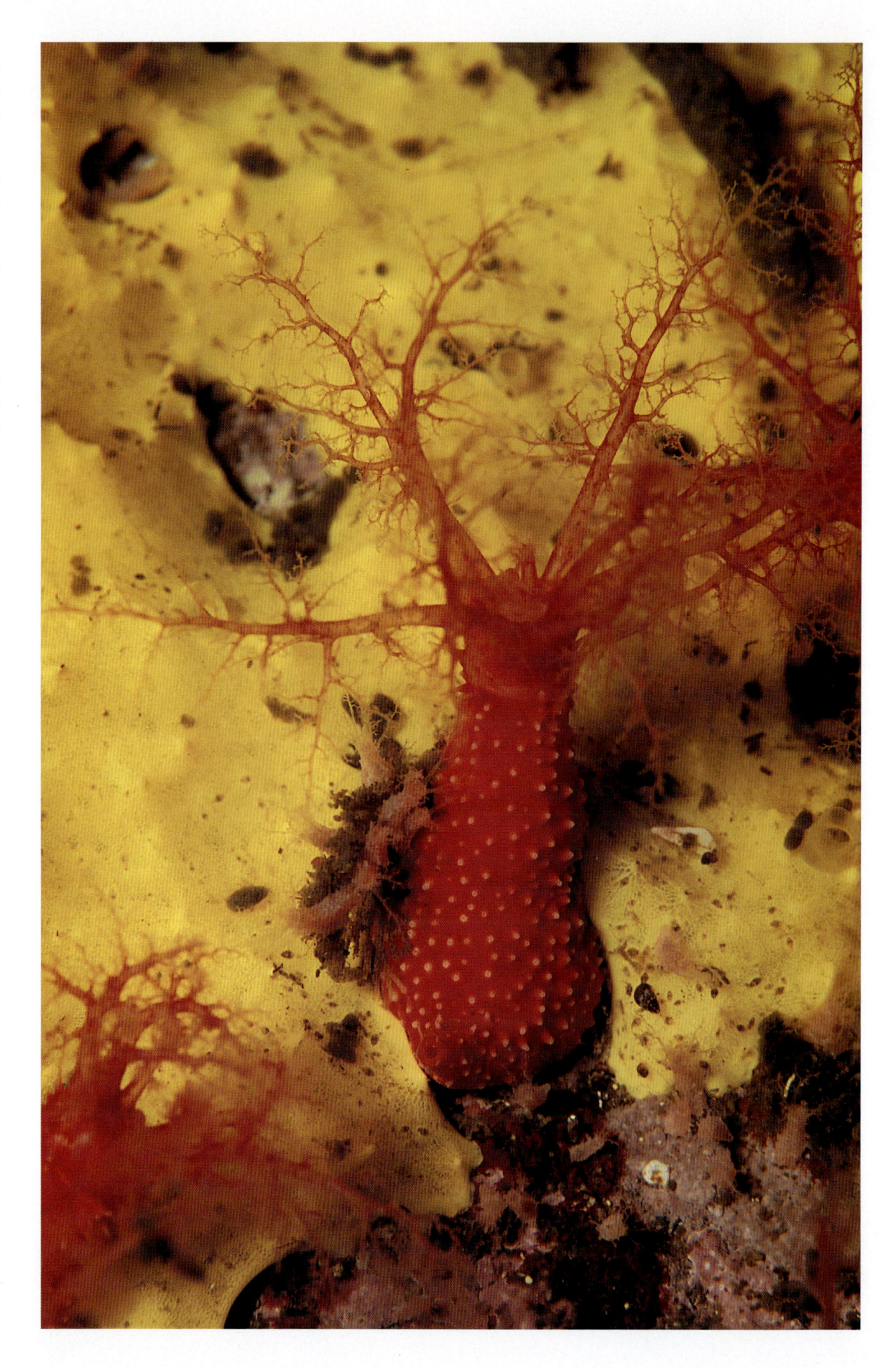

ECHINODERMS 111

11

Bryozoans

BRYOZOANS are known as lace corals or moss animals. On the steep rock walls of the fiords they are among the dominant sessile organisms, particularly on outcrops or in areas subject to a light water current. However, the gentle currents within the fiords in which the lace corals grow are no match for currents generated by the fins of unwary divers; the careless flip of a foot can easily create a current capable of destroying a colony. Undisturbed by this sort of unwelcome attention, a colony may live from one to ten years or more. Growth is seasonal, but more vigorous in spring, when reproduction occurs.

Bryozoans are colonial organisms, each colony being made up of a number of zooids. The colony may be flat and encrusting, dendroid, massive, or erect and lace-like in form. Stoloniferous colonies have erect or creeping stolons made up of modified zooids which give a jointed appearance to the stolon. Unmodified zooids attach themselves by their posterior end to the stolon. The zooids within a colony communicate by passage of coelomic fluid through pores in the walls of the zooecium. Some non-stoloniferous colonies possess a colonial nervous system.

The zooids themselves have two main parts: the zooecium or body wall, and the polypide which can be retracted into the zooecium. The polypide consists of a ring of tentacles around the mouth and a U-shaped digestive tube which terminates in an anus.

In some species a calcareous trapdoor closes behind the polypide after it seeks shelter in the zooecium. They feed on organic matter in the water, small particles being trapped by cilia on the tentacles and passed to the mouth. In some species a modified zooid sweeps backwards and forwards over the colony like a tiny wiper blade and serves a similar function. Another modified zooid is equipped with predatory moveable lower jaw and grows on the end of a long stalk. This zooid prevents the colony from being overgrown by other animals.

Lace corals exhibit a variety of growth forms and a range of colour which makes identification by the non-specialist almost impossible. They are well represented in Fiordland, sometimes abundantly so. So far, according to Dennis Gordon (NIWA), 170 species have been recorded within the fiords, with many additional species present on the outer coast to shelf depths. Within the

(Right) *Amastigia* sp. and *Crisia* sp. **Bryozoans are colonial organisms and grow in a variety of shapes.**

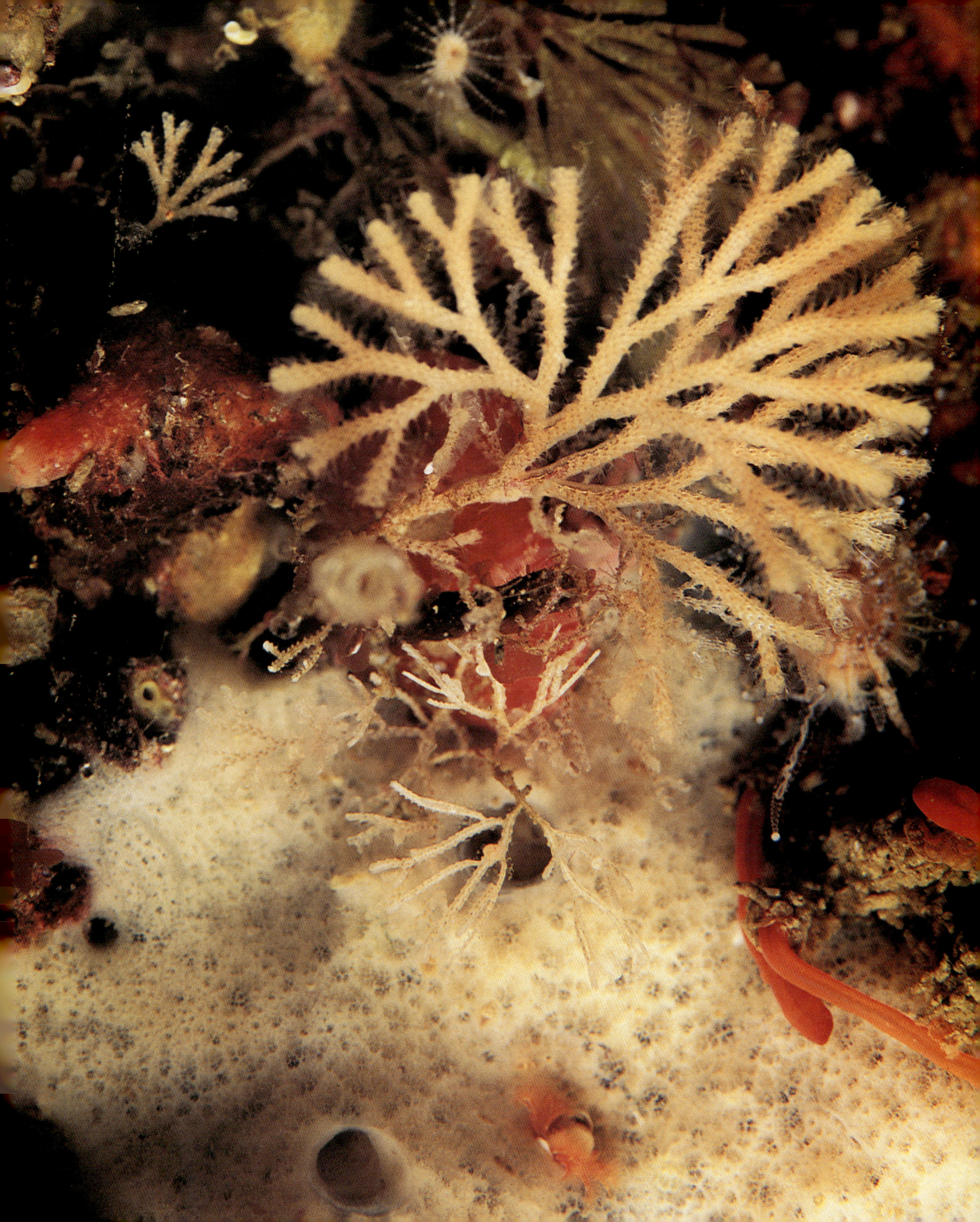

(Right) Colonial bryozoans may be flat and encrusting, dendroid, massive or erect and lacelike in growth form.

(Opposite, Middle) *Hippellozooia novaezelandiae*. The delicate skeletal structure gives rise to the common name 'lace coral'.

(Opposite, Lower) *Muropetraliella ligulata*. Bryozoans often dominate on newly available surfaces and are particularly common on the fiord sills.

fiords, bryozoans occur mainly on the rock walls, but the sills at the entrances to the fiords also provide habitats for bryozoans, including the sediments that may occur on the sills. Of those fiords that have been fairly well sampled, Milford Sound has the highest number of bryozoan species recorded to date, with over 90 species, with Breaksea Sound recording more than 60 species. Over 40 species of bryozoans have been recorded from most of the other fiords, but these numbers are conservative, and many more species can be expected, including new ones.

As demonstrated by researchers from the University of Otago using slate panels in Deep Cove at Doubtful Sound, bryozoans tend to dominate surfaces newly available for colonisation. In this situation, the two-dimensional encrusters flourish first, spreading concentrically across the substrate to form mostly circular patches from 5 to about 35 millimetres diameter, depending on the species. They come in many colours, ranging from semi-transparent or white (*Crepidacantha, Exochella, Fenestrulina, Microporella, Opaeophora*), through buff or pale brown (*Gregarinidra, Steginoporella, Valdemunitella*), to yellow (*Bitectipora, Figularia*), brownish-orange (*Mucropetraliella*), orange (*Escharoides, Foveolaria, Smittina, Smittoidea*), or reddish (*Eurystomella*). Species of these genera reproduce relatively quickly, usually within a few months, and the mostly intensely coloured embryos and larvae dotting the colonies are visible to the unaided eye underwater.

These bryozoan encrusters, however, eventually become dominated by larger (i.e. three-dimensional) sponges and ascidians and other organisms.

Those bryozoans that are bushy and erect and grow outwards from the substratum can coexist fairly well, as they require only a very small attachment surface. These include thin, jointed-stemmed, white colonies of *Cellaria tenuirostris*; bushy orange colonies of *Cribricellina cribraria* and *Orthoscuticella species*, whose branches are made up of chains of tiny segments of one or two zooids; hairy-looking, bushy colonies of *Cellaria pilosa* (pink), *Margaretta barbata* (orange), and *Rhabdozoum wilsoni* (white); small white colonies of intricately curling *Emma* species; orange *Caberea* species, whose branches fan out, often in one plane; and whitish-transparent *Scrupocellaria* and *Tricellaria*.

Out on the fiord entrance sills, where water movement can be quite substantial, coral-like colonies of purplish *Adeonellopsis* form intricate thickets of flattened staghorn-like branches. Large colonies can reach the size of a football and many colonies can cover a large area. In sediments on the sills or ledges within fiords are small, circular colonies of a remarkable genus of Bryozoa (*Otionella*) that has the power of colonial movement. Bristles around the perimeter of the lentil-like colonies can lurch colonies along towards light or help extricate themselves from temporary covering of sandy sediment.

The bryozoans in Fiordland waters are mostly those that occur around much of New Zealand, but there are some species that are rare or absent elsewhere on the coastline that are otherwise quite characteristic of Australia. In Doubtful Sound, studies with experimental panels have turned up several species new to science.

Ascidians

LIKE sponges, ascidians are not a significant feature of the Fiordland benthos. Although invertebrates, ascidians have the rudimentary beginnings of a notochord, a vertebrate characteristic. Their ecological niche is not dissimilar to sponges and bryozoans. They have an extremely reduced biodiversity within the fiords. Only seven species were found in any abundance from 195 species collected during an exercise designed to provide equal sampling effort across plant and animal groups. In any one fiord only a few species were common, and in general the biomass of ascidians was small throughout the fiords. Like sponges, and indeed other encrusting organisms, ascidians are found localised around black coral stands and in areas of accelerated current.

Chris Battershill notes that the commonest species in any fiord here is the thin encrusting colonial ascidian *Didemnum candidum* which occurs in a variety of colours from white through pink to orange. Other encrusting species included the more colourful *Leptoclinides* and *Botrylloides* species which are most commonly found around the bases of black coral trees and macroalgae. Solitary ascidians, primarily *Cnemidocarpa bicornuta*, are common on the outer fiord walls.

As with the sponge fauna, ascidian species found in Fiordland have affinities with northern warm temperate assemblages and only two species were found which may be undescribed. While this group was represented by only a few species and biomass was in general small, some sites did support prolific growth. In these instances, didemnid species were seen to grow as if dripping like molten wax down the fiord wall. In some places this cascade of living ascidian was substantial. This mode of growth has been observed in other localities and appears to be an asexual reproductive strategy where the animal buds off extruded tissue which then can settle further down the wall. In some cases large pieces break off and may be carried to other ledges by currents. This activity occurs in the late summer months.

According to Chris Battershill, of all the encrusting marine organism groups, ascidians appear with the lowest diversity and have generally low biomass in any area. Once again the reasons for this are obscure. It could be related to limited food supply or the lack of larval supply. Immediately outside the fiords, ascidians occur in great profusion, but their distribution wanes dramatically

(Right) ***Didemnum candidum*. Ascidians resemble sponges, but are very different in structure and lack spicules.**

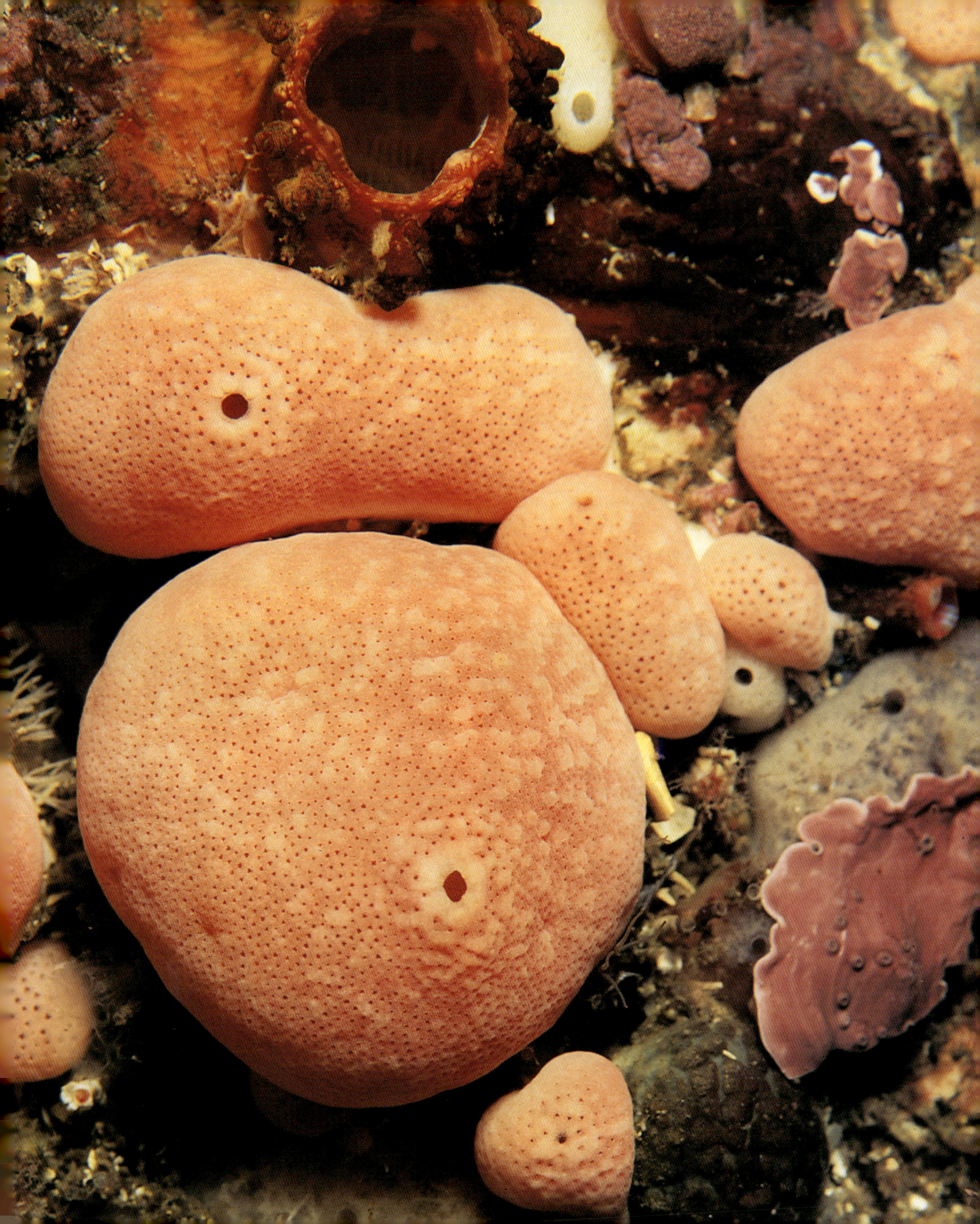

towards the head of a fiord. Unlike sponges, ascidian larvae can achieve dispersal over relatively long distances and can remain viable for long periods of time. Their inability to disperse into fiords would not appear to be a factor in limiting population establishment on fiord walls. There is clearly much to be learned about the ecology of Fiordland's subtidal marine ecosystem.

Salps are pelagic tunicates which differ from the sessile ascidians in having the buccal and atrial siphons at opposite ends of the body. The exhalant water current is used as a means of locomotion. Cigar-shaped colonies of *Pyrosoma atlanticum* are extremely common in Fiordland and generally range in size from 100 to 200 millimetres in length. *Pyrosoma* are best seen at night because of their spectacular eerie blue luminescence. Together with other bioluminescent organisms they make up a spectacular and unforgettable display: light rainfall on the surface waters causes thousands of planktonic animals to flash.

(Left and Below) **Solitary and colonial ascidian species are found in Fiordland, but they rarely, if ever, dominate the cliff community. Assemblages shown here include the ascidians** *Cnemidocarpa bicornuta*, *Didemnum candidum* **and the sponges** *Clathrina coriacea*, *Axinella tricalcyformis*, **spaghetti worm and hydroids.**

(Opposite page, Top) **The encrusting ascidian** *Didemnum densum* **is the most common species in Fiordland.**

(Opposite, Lower Left) **An unidentified encrusting ascidian.**

(Opposite, Lower Right) *Cnemidocarpa bicornuta*. **The body of an ascidian or seasquirt is encased in a tough leathery tunic that gives rise to its alternative name, tunicates.**

(Right) **Colonial red ascidian. Ascidians in a variety of colours are usually found localised around black coral stands, although only seven species occur in any abundance in the fiords.**

(Opposite page, Top Left) *Oplidium*, **new species.**

(Opposite, Top Right) **Assemblage including the ascidians** *Cnemidocarpa bicornuta* **at top,** *Didemnum candidum* **and the sponge** *Clathrina coriacea.*

(Opposite, Lower Left) **Wax ascidian undergoing asexual reproduction resembles molten wax dripping down the fiord wall.**

(Opposite, Lower Right) *Pseudodistoma* **sp.**

ASCIDIANS 121

(Right) **Exhalant opening of the tunicate** *Cnemidocarpa bicornuta*, **surrounded by** *Botrylloides* **sp.**

(Below) *Didemnum candidum.*

(Opposite page) **Salps are pelagic tunicates whose bioluminescence can provide a spectacular sight after dark in the fiords.**

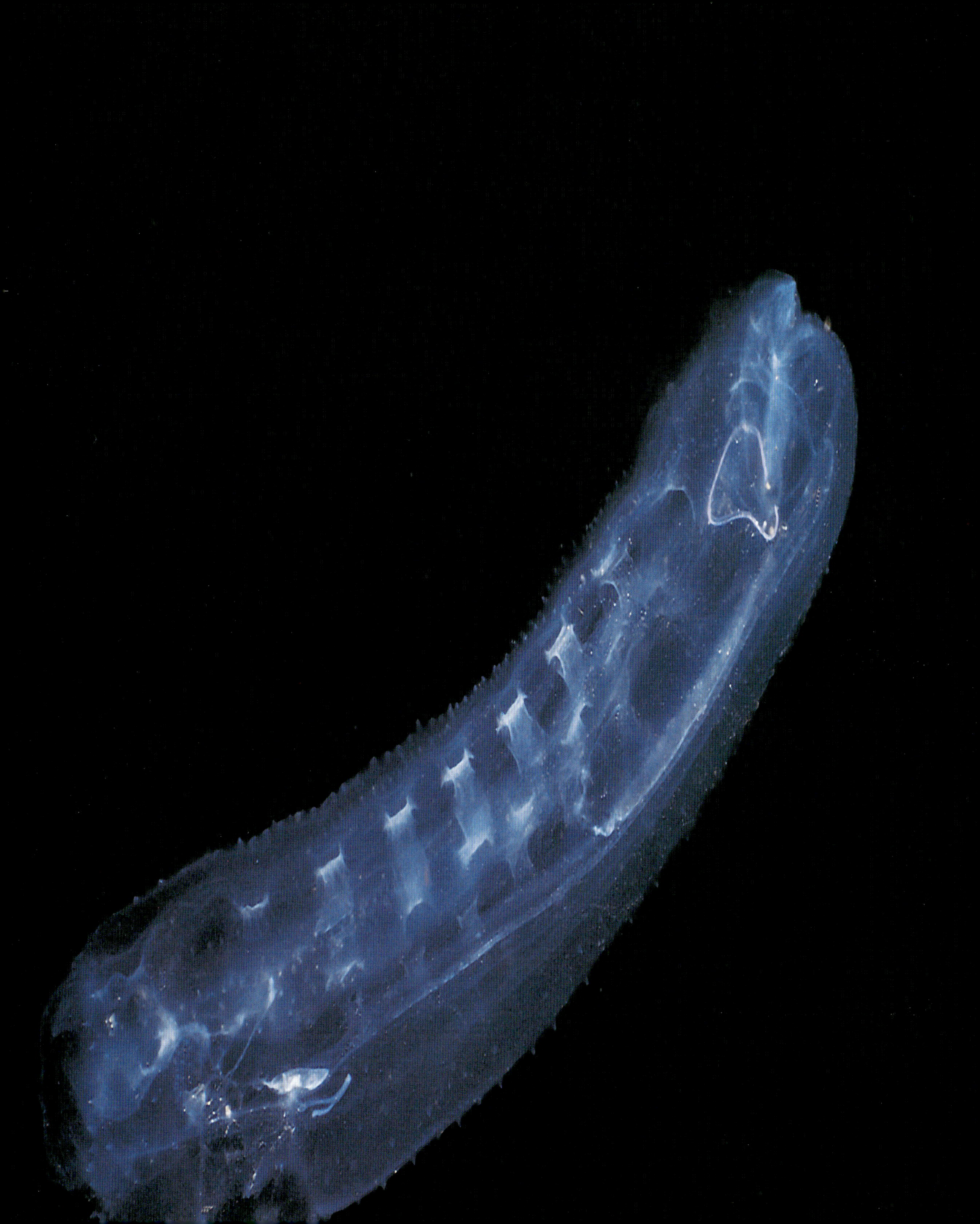

13

Fishes

FIORDLAND fishes were among the first New Zealand animals to be collected and described by the naturalists who accompanied James Cook on his voyages of discovery in the 18th Century. After four months exploring Antarctic waters in 1773, Cook anchored the *Resolution* alongside Astronomer Point in Pickersgill Harbour, Dusky Sound. Here Cook stayed for several weeks, replenishing his supplies while the scientists on board surveyed the area. Here too, Cook established New Zealand's first brewery, perhaps inspiring the name Pickersgill Harbour – after Richard Pickersgill, described as "*…a good officer, but liking ye grog…*".

The naturalists on board, Johann and George Forster, with the assistance of Anders Sparrman, soon collected and drew many fish species. Unfortunately none of the specimens have survived in collections; however, the detailed notes and paintings made were used as the basis for scientific descriptions by other European ichthyologists. Some of this work was published only after considerable difficulty and strife by Bloch & Schneider (1801) and Liechtenstein (1874). The paintings eventually found their way to the British Museum (Natural History) London, but many of these were not published until the bicentennary of Cook's expedition in 1968.

Our visit to Ship Cove in Pickersgill Harbour during the 1993 Museum of New Zealand fish expedition, exactly 220 years after Cook, provided the opportunity for us to collect specimens of the species described by the Forsters, including (amongst others) moki *Latridopsis ciliaris*, scorpionfish *Scorpaena papillosus*, butterfly perch *Caesioperca lepidoptera* and the weedfish *Notoclinus fenestratus*. A short walk to Lake Forster enabled us to collect the galaxiid *Galaxias fasciatus*, but not the giant kokopu *G. argenteus* described by Sparrman in his journal as:

> …a small but new and scaleless pike, patterned as though with hieroglyphics, was caught, and made a pleasing reward for our trouble…

With the exception of some visual fish surveys carried out in Milford and Doubtful Sounds, to date there has been little fish research in the fiords since the visit by Cook. Because of this, the Museum carried out extensive

(Right) **Telescope fish *Mendosoma lineatum*, form huge schools and are one of the dominant pelagic species in middle and outer fiord areas.**

124 FIORDLAND UNDERWATER

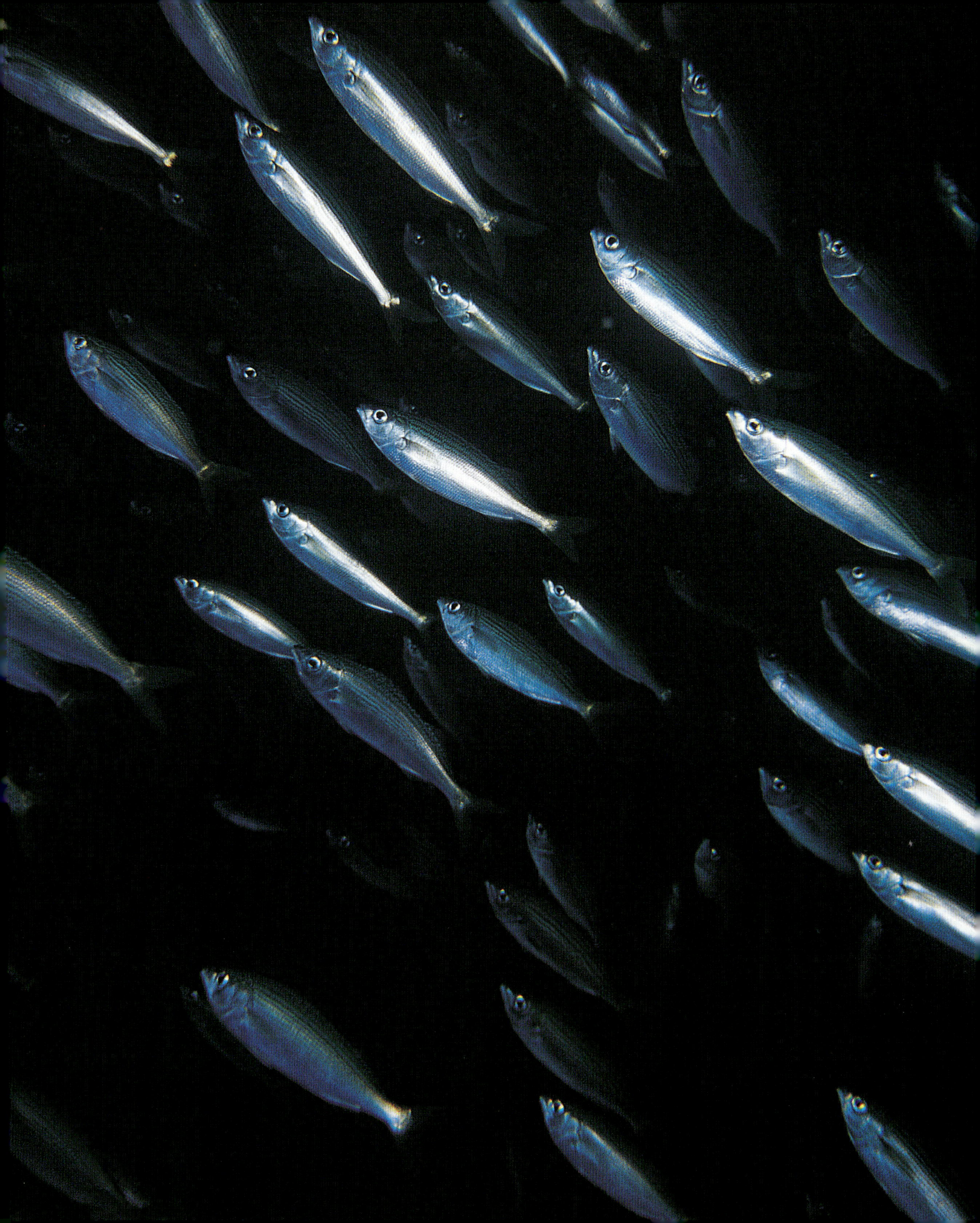

(Right) **Butterfly perch** *Caesioperca lepidoptera* often adopt nocturnal coloration because of the low light conditions and school in areas where the coral and sponge growth is high.

(Opposite page, Top) **Butterfly perch** *Caesioperca lepidoptera* are the visually dominant demersal fishes throughout the fiords.

(Opposite, Middle) **The wavy line perch** *Lepidoperca tasmanica*, usually found at depths of 100m or more off the coast, occurs as shallow as 6m in the two southernmost fiords.

(Opposite, Lower) **Opal fish** *Hemercoetes* spp., are common on sandy shelves and ledges.

126 FIORDLAND UNDERWATER

fish-collecting and survey work throughout the fiords in order to obtain voucher specimens and investigate the biogeography of the ichthyofauna. These fish specimens have been deposited in the fish collection at the Museum of New Zealand in Wellington where they will remain for scientific study, providing important baseline reference material.

The species composition of the fish fauna of Fiordland is essentially the same as that found throughout coastal Otago and southern New Zealand. Fishes such as blue cod *Parapercis colias*, blue moki *Latridopsis ciliaris*, tarakihi *Nemadactylus macropterus*, spiny dogfish *Squalus acanthias*, and red cod *Psuedophycis bachus*, typical of the southern region, are common throughout Fiordland. Species range in size from the 6-metre white shark to the 30-millimetre pygmy sleeper.

The majority of the 180 or so species recorded are widespread in New Zealand waters, with a small component of sub-Antarctic species that are distributed only south of the Chatham Rise, and a few 'northern species' which normally are found north of the Chatham Rise, but occasionally straggle into fiord waters. One feature of the fish fauna that is unusual (as with many invertebrate species) is the presence in shallow water of species otherwise considered deep water fishes and not usually seen by divers.

The phenomenon of deep water species occurring in apparently viable shallow water populations in New Zealand fiords has been recorded for sessile invertebrates (Grange *et al*, 1985) and fishes (Roberts 1989), and more recently also reported in southwestern Tasmania. As yet the phenomenon has not been specifically addressed by detailed survey and analysis, and is not understood. The most spectacular fish examples are the wavy line perch *Lepidoperca tasmanica*, which is found at depths of 10 to 30 metres in the southern fiords, but elsewhere is not known from depths of less than 100 metres, and the splendid perch *Callanthias allporti*, usually recorded only below 25 metres, which can be seen swimming among the wharf piles at Blanket Bay, Doubtful Sound. Spiny sea-dragons *Solegnathus spinossissimus*, a close relative of the sea-horse, and yellow weevers *Parapercis gilliesi* are usually seen only when trawled in coastal waters, but are occasionally observed in diving depths in the fiords.

Fish species diversity within the fiords is generally lowest near the heads of the fiords and increases seawards. Abundance of individual species varies considerably. Spotties *Notolabrus celidotus*, are abundant in the inner fiords but numbers decrease dramatically towards the more exposed outer coast. The reverse pattern is found among weed-dwelling or herbivorous species, such as banded wrasse *Notolabrus fucicola*, and butterfish *Odax pullus*, reflecting the distribution of algae. Jock stewart or sea-perch *Helicolenus percoides*, can be found resting on ledges or any available flat space throughout the fiords.

The visually dominant demersal species such as butterfly perch *Caesioperca lepidoptera*, scarlet wrasse *Pseudolabrus miles*, girdled wrasse *Notolabrus cinctus*, and blue cod *Parapercis colias*, increase in abundance both seawards and with depth. Girdled wrasse are extremely territorial and will defend their area from even the largest intruder, not hesitating to attack divers, often inflicting painful nips to exposed portions of anatomy (fortunately in Fiordland, few portions of the anatomy are exposed). This diver-positive response is typical of many species, particularly wrasses and blue cod, in a pristine area where spearfishing fortunately is uncommon. Small schools of fish will follow divers closely, giving a false impression of total numbers. Remote-operated video cameras have been experimented with by Euan Harvey (Otago University) and Ken Grange (NIWA) in an attempt to validate visual census methods.

The most common fishes are not the visually dominant demersal species, which are seen individually or in loose schools around the boulders and coral, but the small, at first seemingly insignificant cryptic species. These cryptic

(Left) **Blue cod** *Parapercis colias* populations are lower in the more accessible fiords.

(Below Left) **Banded wrasse** *Notolabrus fucicola* increase in abundance towards the outer fiords, where algae growth is most prolific.

(Below) **Sea-horses** *Hippocampus abdominalis* occur in low numbers.

(Opposite page, Top) **The southern bastard cod** *Pseudophycis barbata* lurks in caves and overhangs in the outer fiord areas.

(Opposite, Middle) **Blue cod** *Parapercis colias*, common throughout the fiords, are a popular target of commercial and recreational fisheries.

(Opposite, Lower) **The splendid perch** *Callanthias alporti* is usually found in pairs near large caves and overhangs.

(Right) **The tiny spectacularly coloured bluedot triplefin** *Notoclinops caerulepunctus* **(45 mm) is easy to miss because of its size.**

(Below) **Rockfishes** *Acanthoclinus* **spp. are nocturnal predators, spending the daylight hours under rocks or in crevices.**

130 FIORDLAND UNDERWATER

fish species are extremely common in the fiords and, as with the larger demersal species, they increase in number and diversity seawards. These fishes are benthic or bottom-dwelling, and difficult to see among the profusion of sessile organisms where the males defend communal nests and territories from other males, as well as from other fish predators.

Most important are the triplefins, our commonest and most valuable reef fishes, which are found throughout New Zealand. On the outer coast and near the fiord entrances the common triplefin *Forsterygion lapillum*, is found in very high densities. However, this proliferation pales into insignificance in the inner and middle sections of the fiords where it is sometimes found at densities of hundreds per square metre.

Another common fish within the fiords is the estuarine triplefin *Grahamina nigripenne*. This species is found on mudflats and occasionally along the rocky sides of the fiords at the freshwater/seawater interface, especially near river deltas. Near the fiord entrances and in the middle to outer zones of the fiords, schools of thousands of oblique swimming triplefins *Obliquichthys maryannae*, are seen hanging in the shadows cast by the bands of algae or in the middle zones, where algae is absent, below rocky overhangs, while on the rock-face itself hundreds of yellow-black triplefins *Forsterygion flavonigrum* defend territories.

Extremely effective camouflage coloration conceals the scorpionfish *Scorpaena papillosus*, which will only reluctantly move a short distance when disturbed. The 100 to 150 millimetre-long mottled triplefin *Forsterygion malcolmi*, is seen among rocks, particularly near steep overhangs where the eggs are laid on bare surfaces and protected by the male. Even closer investigation of the rock walls will reveal the smaller cryptic species such as blue eye triplefins *Notoclinops segmentatus*, and blue dot triplefins *N. caerulepunctus*, which reach a length of only 60 to 70 millimetres.

Living beneath rocks and in holes are several species of rockfishes *Acanthoclinus* spp., rockling *Gaidropsarus novaezelandiae* and clingfishes, Family Gobiesocidae. The rarely observed but relatively common urchin clingfish *Dellichthys morelandi*, lives beneath the spines of the common urchin *Evechinus*, and can be seen by quickly lifting a sea-urchin off the rock, as the clingfish swims rapidly to the next available host urchin.

Divers will be rewarded by careful approach to a boulder field or crevice by a glimpse of one of our most spectacular fishes, the splendid rockfish *Acanthoclinus matti*, perching at the entrance to its lair. Several other species of fish are common but live deep within crevices. The use of a torch will reveal the lurking conger eel *Conger verreauxi*, or the rock cod *Lotella rhacinus*, but our smallest New Zealand vertebrate, the undescribed pygmy sleeper *Thallaseleotris* n.sp. living in the back of mud-filled crevices, can be collected only by using special ichthyocides and live fish have never been seen.

Larger holes and caves provide shelter for small schools of common roughy *Paratrachichthys trailli* and the occasional splendid perch *Callanthias allporti* or banded perch *Hypoplectrodes huntii*. On open areas of shelly sediment the opalfish *Hemerocoetes* spp., blends perfectly with the background, and is only seen when a diver approaches too close, as it darts away to a new position.

Throughout most of the fiords, spiny dogfish *Squalus acanthias* are found at depths of 20 to 25 metres, barely visible at the edge of the gloom as they carefully avoid divers, while occasionally a small carpet shark *Cephaloscyllium isabellum* may cruise past. Hagfish *Eptatretus cirrhatus* abound on the deep muddy floors of the fiords.

At many places in the fiords vast schools of telescope fish *Mendosoma lineatum*, patrol in the current. At times they are so dense as to block out the light. We have encountered massive schools in Nancy Sound and at The Gut in Doubtful Sound. Telescope fish are named after their highly protrusile mouth parts which they use to pluck food items out of the plankton. Juvenile specimens are sometimes found living inside salps or other soft-bodied organisms. At certain times of the year large schools of other pelagic species, such as jack mackerel *Trachurus* spp., can be observed inside the fiords.

Only one species of fish, a brotula, is known to be endemic to Fiordland. The Fiordland brotula *Fiordichthys slartibartfasti*, was first discovered in 1993 by divers from the Museum of New Zealand Te Papa Tongarewa, who collected two specimens. This fish represents a previously unknown genus and was named after Slartibartfast, a character who designed fiords in the Douglas Adams novel *The Hitchhiker's Guide to the Galaxy*. Email correspondence with Douglas Adams subsequently revealed the curious coincidence that the paper describing the fish (Paulin 1994) was accepted on Adams' 42nd birthday. Of more significance to *Galaxy* aficionados is the vital fact that on a second collecting trip in 1995, one of the two additional specimens we collected was at fish sampling station number 42.

The Fiordland brotula is found in holes and crevices at depths of 10 to 12 metres and reaches a maximum size of around 220 millimetres. Nothing is known of the biology of the species; however, because of its strong teeth and jaws it is thought to be an active predator.

Other related fishes within the family are nocturnal and, unlike most fishes, give birth to live young. To date (1998) only four specimens are known. There is a possibility that this species is another deep water emergent and more specimens may yet be discovered in other regions of New Zealand living at greater depths than can be reached by scuba diving.

Commercial species are usually taken within the fiords when stormy weather prevents fishing vessels from venturing to the outer coasts. The main species targeted are blue cod *Parapercis colias*, and groper *Polyprion oxygeneios*. Culinary tastes have changed dramatically in the years since the European exploration and settlement of New Zealand. The fish stocks were plentiful, yet the settlers were nostalgic for home: Robert Paulin (1889)

(Left) **The brotula *Fiordichthys slartibartfasti* (220 mm) is known from just four specimens collected in the region.**

(Below) **The oblique swimming triplefin *Obliquichthys maryannae* is rarely seen at rest.**

(Opposite, Top) **Blue-eyed triplefins *Notoclinops segmentatus*, are common in Fiordland and elsewhere on the New Zealand coastline.**

(Opposite, Middle) **Mottled triplefin *Forsterygion malcolmi* (125 mm), occupy areas of bare rock where the males defend nest sites.**

(Opposite, Lower) **A male yellow-black triplefin *Forsterygion flavonigrum* in its breeding coloration.**

FISHES 133

(Right) **Leatherjackets** *Parika scaber* **are not common and are usually seen only in the middle and outer fiords.**

(Opposite page, Top) **Witch** *Arnoglossus scapha* **occur on sandy or muddy ledges.**

(Opposite, Middle) **Eye of a carpet shark,** *Cephaloscyllum isabellum.*

(Opposite, Lower) **Leatherjacket** *Parika scaber* **is easily identified by the stout erectile spine on the top of the head.**

(Opposite, Lower Right) **The oblique swimming triplefin** *Obliquichthys maryannae.*

commented on groper (now regarded as a prime species):

> The groper or hapuka is very common on these coasts; it is generally caught about 10 or 20 lbs. in weight, sometimes much heavier... They are something like a cod in appearance; their flesh is white and very solid. Groper cutlet is not bad by any means when one is hungry or has not tasted fish for some time. They are a coarse fish, and about the cheapest sold in the Dunedin market. I cannot say I care much for them myself.

He also considered rock lobster to be "very insipid" in comparison with the English lobster. This attitude was prevalent throughout much of the colony of New Zealand, particularly among the Scottish settlers of Otago and was the principle reason for the establishment of one of the world's first Marine Research Laboratories at Portobello, Dunedin (now part of the Otago University Department of Marine Science). This was done not to study the biology of the local fish and effect of fisheries, but as an attempt to introduce marine species such as herring and turbot from Europe, as had been done successfully with the freshwater trout and salmon.

Fortunately, despite considerable efforts, none of these species became established, although many fish were reared to adult size and released into Otago waters.

(Right) **Jock stewart or sea-perch** *Helicolenus percoides*, is one of the more common benthic fishes found throughout the fiords.

(Below and Opposite) **The scorpionfish** *Scorpaena papillosa*, a close relative of the jock stewart, is difficult to see against the sponge-covered rock wall and the bryozoa.

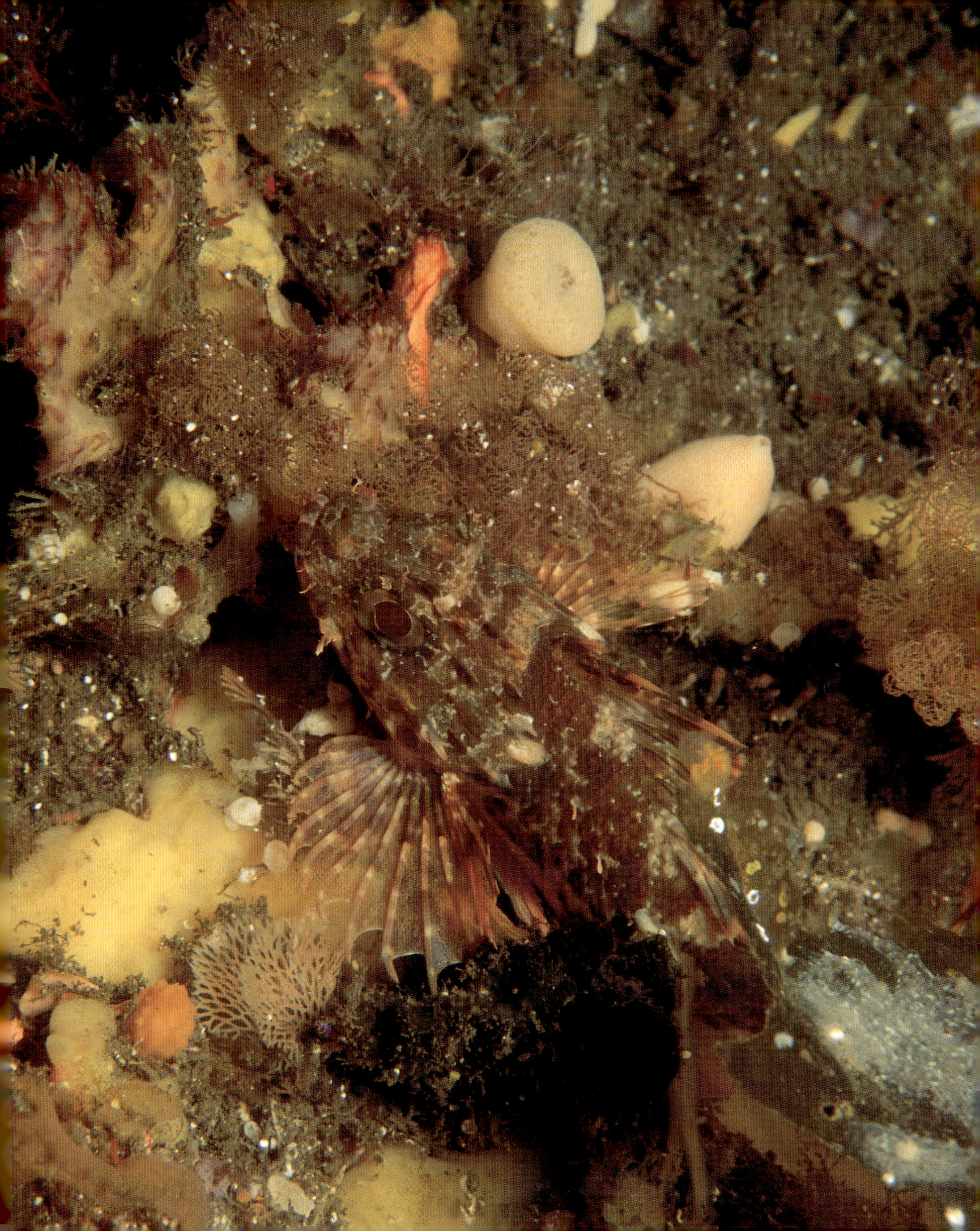

(Top Left) **Hagfish** *Eptatretis cirrhatus*, may occasionally be seen in shallow depths but are more common in the deep muddy fiord basins below diving depth.

(Top Right) **The hagfish is a scavenger, feeding on dead fishes and other organisms.**

(Below Right) **Body proportions of the telescope fish change with age: adults are deeper-bodied than juveniles.**

(Below) **With the absence of spearfishing in most of the fiords, large fish such as the trumpeter** *Latris lineata* **are relatively tame and will often approach divers.**

(Opposite page) **The yellow-black triplefin** *Forsterygion flavonigrum.*

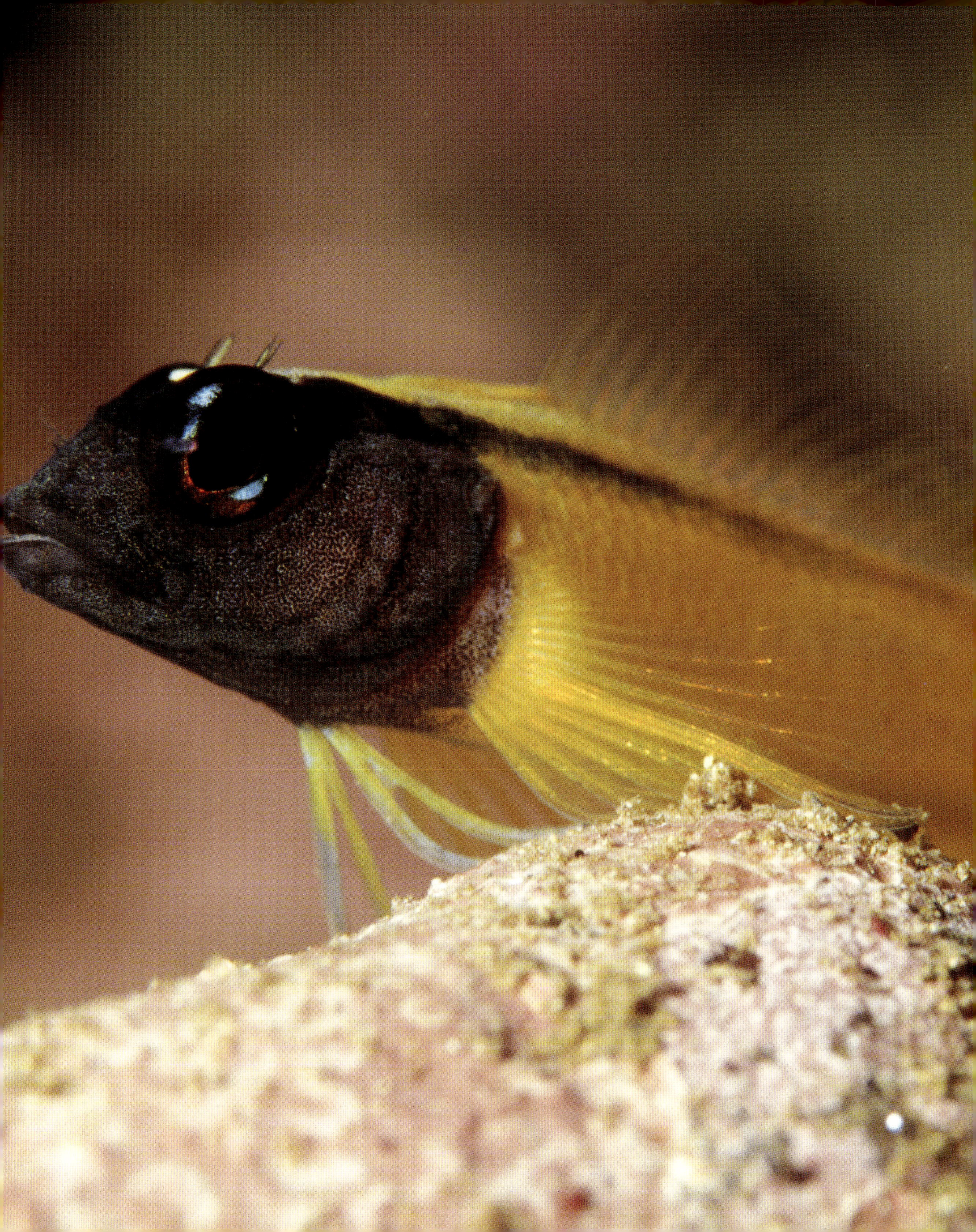

(Right) **The spiny sea-dragon *Solegnathus spinossissimus* is a deep water emergent.**

(Below) **The variable triplefin *Forsterygion varium*, named by naturalists with Captain Cook in the 18th century for its 'variable' colour pattern. Research has since shown that these colour patterns represent several different species.**

(Opposite page) **Overhangs and crevices are home to the banded perch *Hypoplectrodes huntii*.**

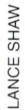

140   FIORDLAND UNDERWATER

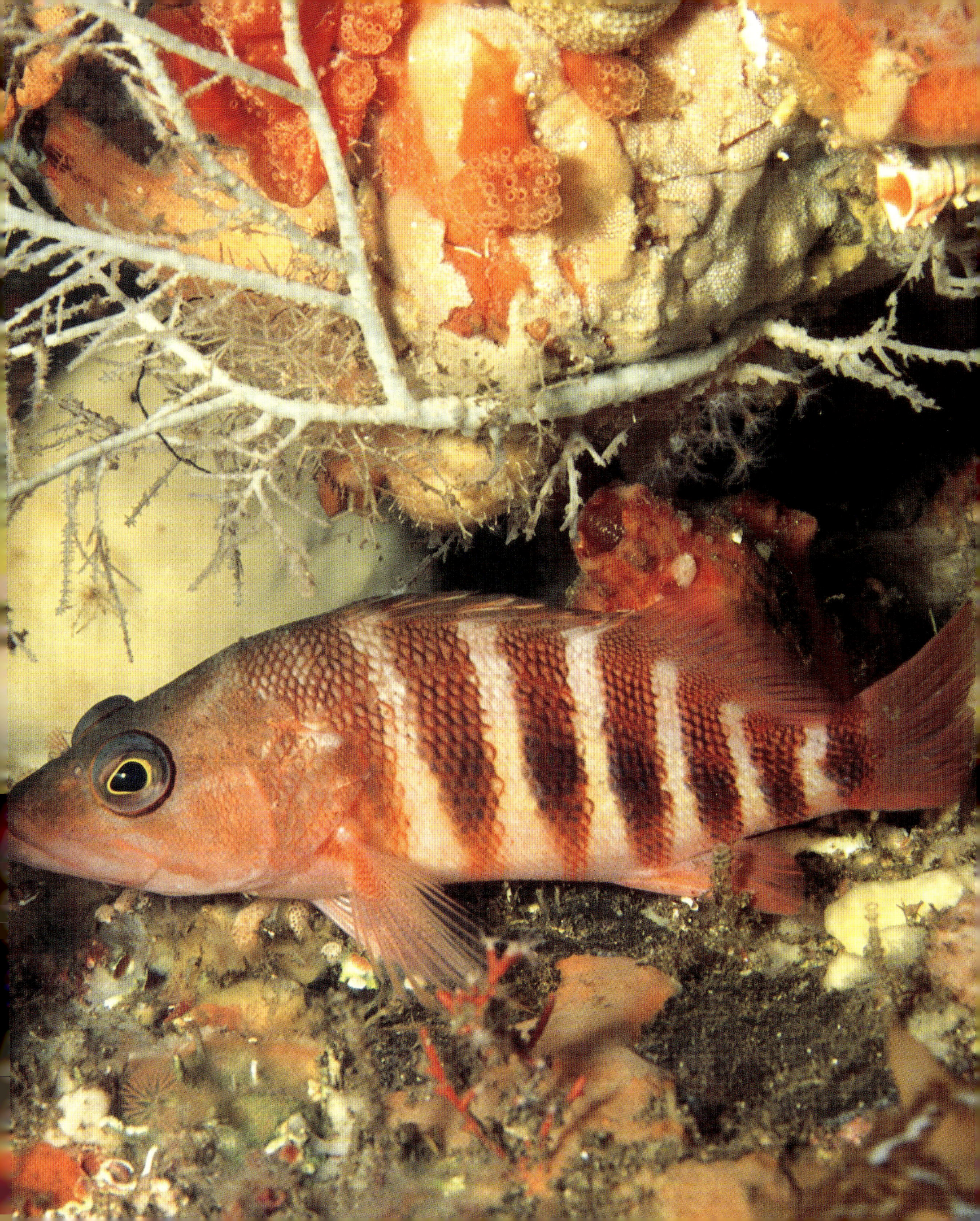

14

Other Marine Vertebrates

MARINE mammals are regular Fiordland visitors and several species, notably fur seals and bottlenose dolphins, are resident within the fiords.

Fur seals *Arctocephalus forsteri* are becoming more common around New Zealand as their numbers gradually increase after near extermination in the early 1800s. Fur seals are usually seen resting onshore in areas of exposed rocky coast where offshore reefs give some protection from heavy seas. When James Cook explored southern New Zealand in the 18th century, he found seals "innumerable", and noted the ease by which they could be killed for their meat, skins and blubber. Harvesting began in the 1800s and by 1810 over 10,000 seal skins per year were being taken. By 1825 the seals were virtually exterminated. Despite this harvest, the species was not given a formal scientific description until 1828.

For most of the 19th century fur seals were rare around the New Zealand coast. In 1889 Robert Paulin's only comment was: "…a few seals may still be found around the rocks."

Numbers increased steadily, to reach an estimated total New Zealand population of 40,000 in the 1970s (King 1983). Today the population is still increasing and figures of 55,000-plus are quoted, but there has not been a detailed census for years. In some northern areas numbers are increasing (as much as by 10 to 15 percent annually in some locations) and breeding has been reported in the southern North Island, but at Open Bay Islands in South Westland, Hugh Best (Department of Conservation) has found numbers are relatively stable.

Although fur seals are being studied in various areas of New Zealand, there has been little work done in Fiordland, where most of the breeding colonies are found.

Breeding rookeries are located on offshore islands near the entrances to many of the fiords and on exposed headlands along the outer coast. Solitary individuals, usually juveniles, may be seen throughout the fiords. Breeding takes place between October and March. The adult bulls, which attain weights of up to 185 kg, arrive at the rookeries between October and early December. Rookeries are already occupied by subadults, yearlings and young females which will probably have wintered over at the site. Adult cows feed intensively offshore during late spring and early summer and begin arriving

(Right) **New Zealand fur seal *Arctocephalus forsteri* abound in rookeries on rocky promontories and islands along the open Fiordland coast.**

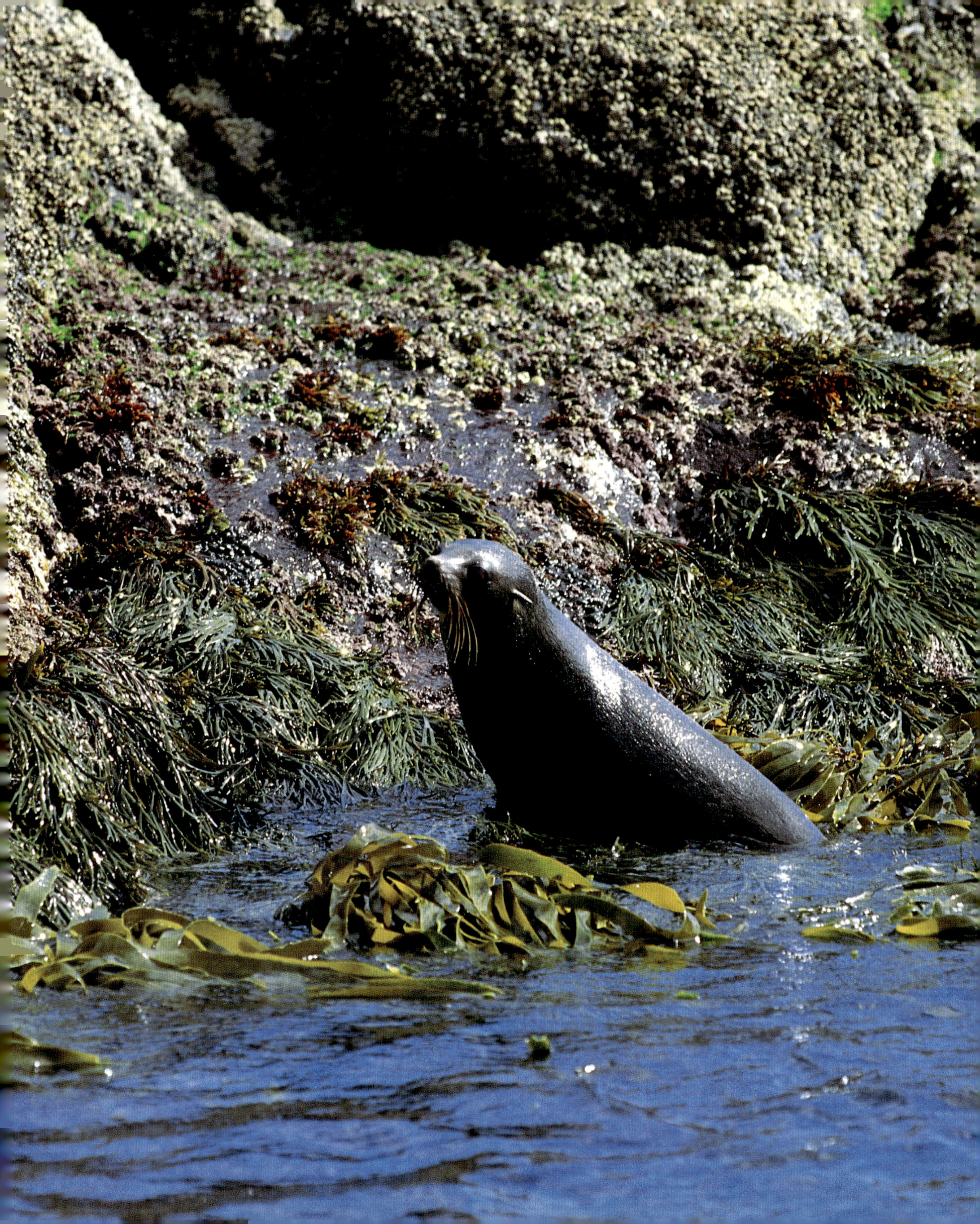

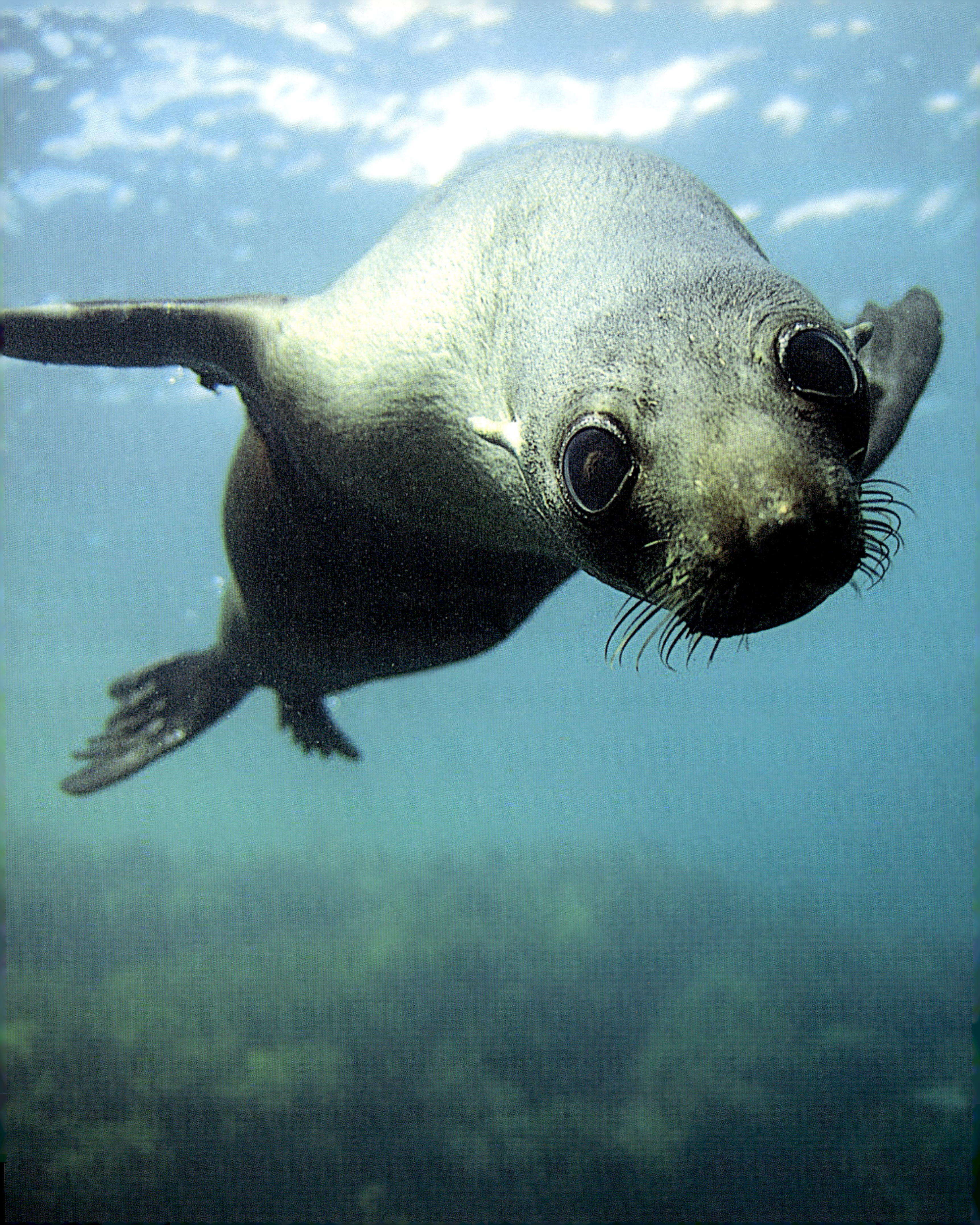

in numbers a few weeks after the males have established territories. Pups are born between mid-November and late January and are about 550 millimetres long and dark black in colour. This changes to the typical silvery grey yearling coloration after the first moult at two months. The female stays with the pup for the first 10 days then begins to make progressively longer feeding trips to sea, returning to the pup every two to five days. Pups are suckled for about a year. By late summer the pups gather in pods and the harem system breaks down as the males return to the sea after spending up to 10 weeks on land without feeding.

Microprocessor depth recorders have been attached to female fur seals by Rob Mattlin and Nick Gales (Victoria University, Wellington and DoC) who found that some fur seals may dive to depths in excess of 100 metres to feed (with a maximum recorded at 238 metres) but most diving is at depths of 30 to 64 metres. The diet comprises mainly squid and octopus with mid-water pelagic fish species such as hoki, jack mackerel, barracouta, myctophids or lantern fish and some other species being taken.

In different regions fur seal diet reflects local prey availability and they are not averse to taking the occasional blue penguin or hand-out. This latter activity can result in their being accused of interfering with commercial fishing. With the onset of extensive hoki fishing off the South Island's west coast, fur seals soon learned that fish could be easily obtained from the open mouth of the large deep water trawls as these were being retrieved. Unfortunately the trawls were often reset if they were not full of fish, resulting in the drowning of any seals inside the net. Changes in fishing practices have greatly reduced the numbers killed accidentally in recent years.

Juvenile fur seals often come and investigate divers. Like small puppies, they will cavort through scuba bubbles, nip fins and generally make a nuisance of themselves, but rarely when the appropriate lens is on the camera.

Our colleague Craig Loveridge was paddling a canoe in Milford Sound when he encountered some splashing. Further investigation revealed a leopard seal *Hydrurga leptonyx* feeding on a fur seal which it had apparently attacked and killed. Craig commented that he felt very vulnerable that close to the water and he beat a hasty retreat. Leopard seals do not appear to be a regular part of the Fiordland fauna but may be encountered from time to time. Also straggling into Fiordland occasionally are Hooker's sea-lions *Phocarctos hookeri* and elephant seals *Mirounga leonina*.

After the decimation of the fur seal population in Fiordland, attention turned to exploitation of whales. The first sizeable land-based whaling station in New Zealand was established in Preservation Inlet by 1829. This station lasted less than 10 years, despite taking between 115 and 176 tons of oil annually. Offshore whaling continued until the mid-19th century. Large whales such as sperm *Physeter catodon* and right whales *Eubalaena australis* were taken but these are rarely seen inside the fiords. Smaller cetaceans such as the common bottlenose dolphin *Tursiops truncatus* are frequently encountered inside the fiords.

The bottlenose dolphin is a relatively large species, attaining five metres in length and is recognised by its very short beak. Colour is grey or grey-green dorsally, merging indistinctly with the white belly. The species is found in cool waters of Australasia, South America, the Caribbean, Mediterranean and northern Atlantic. Little is known of the biology of bottlenose dolphins in New Zealand waters, although they have been extensively studied elsewhere.

Bottlenose dolphins around the New Zealand coast move into sheltered waters such as the Marlborough Sounds in late summer and early autumn. These may only be localised movements rather than migration. In Fiordland a small population of around 100 animals is

(Left) Juvenile fur seals are often found throughout the fiords.

(Right) **Fur seal numbers are increasing since near extermination in the 19th century.**

(Below) **The elephant seal *Mirounga leonina*, largest of the pinnipeds, visits Fiordland infrequently.**

(Opposite page) **Sperm whale *Physeter catodon*, seen here off Kaikoura, were hunted off the Fiordland coast until the mid-19th century.**

resident in Doubtful Sound and has been studied by Jamelia Williams (Otago University) and small schools may be seen in other fiords.

Gaskin (1972) reported that in Milford Sound, schools of bottlenose dolphins with very young calves moved to the head of the sound in late summer. During the day most of the adults appeared to go out to sea or the outer portion of the sound to feed, leaving at least one adult to remain with the calves. As the calves grew larger, they began to accompany the adults on the daily feeding trips, finally leaving the sound altogether. During winter, only an occasional adult would be seen.

There are so many good books on New Zealand bird life that it would be superfluous to write much about them here. And while all seabirds are intimately connected with the sea, penguins spend more time actually in it and therefore get pride of place in this brief discussion.

Two penguins are regularly seen in this region: the southern blue penguin *Eudyptes minor* and the endemic Fiordland crested penguin *Eudyptes pachyrhynchus*. Blue penguins are the smallest penguin and are widely distributed around New Zealand's coast in five recognised subspecies. Another subspecies, the fairy penguin, lives around Australia's southern coastline.

Little is known about the southern blue penguin. Other subspecies spend most of their time at sea feeding on small fish, coming ashore mainly to breed and moult. Breeding takes place in late winter and spring. One parent stays with the chicks until they are about 25 days old, at which time both parents hunt during the day, returning at night to feed the chicks and keep them warm. Fledglings leave the nest when they are 48 to 55 days old. Presumably, relieved parents go to sea for a period of intensive feeding and after gaining up to 30 percent of their body weight, come ashore to moult.

Little blues produce a sound out of all proportion to their size. You are unlikely to forget their blood-curdling cry after experiencing it for the first time.

(Right) **Bottlenose dolphins** *Tursiops truncatus* grow to 5m. Several groups of these dolphins appear to be resident within the fiords.

(Opposite page) **Fiordland crested penguins** *Eudyptes pachyrhynchus* once occurred in thousands, but their numbers declined dramatically during the 20th century as a result of introduced mammalian predators taking eggs and chicks.

OTHER MARINE VERTEBRATES *149*

Until recently it was assumed that New Zealand's rarest penguin was the yellow-eyed penguin *Megadyptes antipodes*, which may occasionally straggle into Fiordland. However, while threatened on the South Island mainland, this species seems quite secure in other parts of its range, most notably the Auckland Islands.

Reported by Richard Henry (1903) as occurring "...in thousands", Fiordland crested penguins have undergone a dramatic decline in numbers during the 20th century. A census by the tourist operator Southern Heritage Expeditions and Ian McLean from the University of Canterbury produced a figure of only 2000 to 2500 nests. This places it on a par with the yellow-eyed penguin, but the Fiordland crested penguin is more at risk because the entire population is relatively vulnerable to introduced mammalian predators. The Fiordland crested is arguably the world's rarest penguin.

Fiordland crested penguins nest in burrows on steep hillsides. The parents take it in turns to go to sea and hunt for squid and fish. They usually raise two chicks which start life as little balls of charcoal and white fluff. They become more like the adults in colour and pattern as they grow. The chicks employ a defense system which works against humans but possibly not against dogs or stoats. They are able to projectile vomit with considerable accuracy, but not before they first produce the most appalling din. If you get hit, you can't claim you weren't warned.

(Left) The Fiordland crested penguin *Eudyptes pachyrhynchus*, nests along the outer coast and near the fiord entrances in caves or under tree roots.

(Opposite page) The little blue penguin *Eudyptula minor*, is the most common penguin species in New Zealand. It is found in the middle and outer fiords.

OTHER MARINE VERTEBRATES

15

Topside Biota

WHILE it is Fiordland underwater which constitutes the focus of this book, there are some fascinating plants and animals which inhabit Te Wahipounamu (Fiordland). The decimation of the terrestrial biota serves as a warning for the marine environment. Some 24 of the area's 700-plus native vascular plant species are known solely from Fiordland. One of the more common is *Carex pleiostachys* which forms cushions on rocky coastal platforms. Over 140 species of introduced plants have invaded Fiordland but with a few exceptions most fail to achieve achieve pest status.

Captain Cook was possibly the first European to take advantage of Fiordland's plants. He collected *Lepidium oleraceum* which is now known as Cook's scurvy grass. Poorly named, it is not a grass but a herb, and is now known to be high in vitamin C. How Cook realised it would be useful for its anti-scurvy properties is unknown.

Cook also collected rimu and manuka leaves for the 'first brewery' in New Zealand. He added molasses and wort to produce 'spruce beer'. According to the Swedish scientist Anders Sparrman who accompanied Cook, "after a small amount of rum or arrack had been added, with some brown sugar, and stirred into this really pleasant, refreshing and healthy drink, it bubbled and tasted rather like champagne." Clearly they had been a long time at sea.

The Fiordland forest is a mixture of various beech, podocarp and other species. Silver beech *Nothofagus menziesii* is the predominant beech. Podocarps, so important as a food supply for native birds, include rimu *Dacrydium cupressinum*, Hall's totara *Podocarpus cunninghamii* and kahikatea *Dacrycarpus dacrydioides*. Rata *Metrosideros umbellata* and kamahi *Weinmannia racemosa* also occur as do a bewildering variety of ferns, liverworts and mosses.

Sadly, introduced mammals have wreaked havoc in this otherwise pristine environment. Thus the Australian brush-tailed possum *Trichosurus vulpecula* continues to advance through the bush, preferring to feed on native trees such as southern rata. This alters the structure of the canopy. At ground level, red deer *Cervus elephas*, goats *Capra hircus* and pigs *Sus scrofa* suppress seedling growth by continued browsing. At one stage moose *Alces alces* were introduced but were long thought to have

(Right) **The great English navigator James Cook sighted Fiordland from the *Endeavour* in 1770 (replica ship seen here in Milford Sound, 1996), returning three years later on the *Resolution* to spend six weeks in Dusky Sound. During this visit he collected *Lepidium oleraceum*, discovering its usefulness for its anti-scurvy properties.**

Var 16.31 E
S.W. Bay
Solanders Isle
Bench Island
CAPE SOUTH
Var 16.29 E

died out in the region until May 1998, when the Department of Conservation reported a sighting. Introduced mammals mean that eventually a new equilibrium will eventuate but it will no longer be optimal for the complex communities which used to exist here.

Wherever you anchor in Fiordland waters the sense of isolation is apparent. This is emphasised by the almost total silence. Instead of a cacophony of bird song, you hear isolated calls. The dawn chorus is hardly that any more. Contrast this with the situation Captain Cook and his crew encountered in 1773 on their second voyage to New Zealand, when they entered Fiordland for the first time. George Forster wrote: "Flocks of aquatic birds enlivened the rocky shores, and the whole country resounded with the wild notes of the feathered tribe."

Cook himself recorded that he returned to the boat "with about seven dozen of wild fowl, and two seals; the most of them shot while I was rowing about."

Chris Paulin's great-grandfather Robert Paulin, in his 1889 book *The Wild West Coast of New Zealand – A Summer Cruise in the Rosa* was also impressed by the dawn chorus:

> Next morning at 4.30 a.m. I went on deck, and heard the most extraordinary chorus of singing birds I ever listened to in my life. The air was full of sound as if millions of anvils were being struck with tiny hammers. The effect was indescribable but most enjoyable. It was the bell-birds chanting their morning song; their notes bear no little resemblance to the tinkling of silver bells. Judging from the volume of sound, one would almost think that every tree or bush in the dense forest clothing the mountain sides had one of these feathered warblers for an occupant.

Night-time was spectacular also.

As the darkness came on, the native birds gave us a concert. The soft, prolonged whistle of the kiwi, the weird wailing call of the weka, the clear whistle and harsh screech of the kaka, the still harsher screech of the kakapo, the scream of the penguin, and the plaintiff hoot of the morepork owl were all heard in discordant unison, more or less, through the early hours of the night.

Alas, the introduction of brown and ship rats *Rattus norvegicus*, *R. rattus*, cats *Felis catus*, weasels *Mustela nivalis*, stoats *M. erminea* and ferrets *M. furo* has dealt to that. The steady depredations of these sophisticated mammalian hunters have decimated the bird and insect fauna. These days the night chorus is dominated by the call of the introduced Australian whistling frog *Litoria ewingi*. This was released in a drain in Greymouth in 1875 by a Mr W. Perkins. From this rather cavalier action and humble beginnings, whistling frogs are now well established throughout the West Coast and in parts of Fiordland. No doubt they will continue to spread.

The most endangered species has to be the kakapo *Strigops habroptilus*. The kakapo is the largest parrot in the world and the only flightless parrot species. It has other claims to fame as well. It is nocturnal and is a lek breeder. Lek breeders are those in which males congreg-

(Left) **In Fiordland the New Zealand robin** *Petroica australis* **is confined to remote areas of native bush, but is known to be increasing in numbers in some exotic plantations in the North Island.**

(Below) **The Fiordland skink** *Leiolopisma acrinasum* **is now restricted to offshore islands.**

(Opposite page) **Silver beech** *Nothofagus menziesii* **is the predominant tree throughout the Fiordland rainforest.**

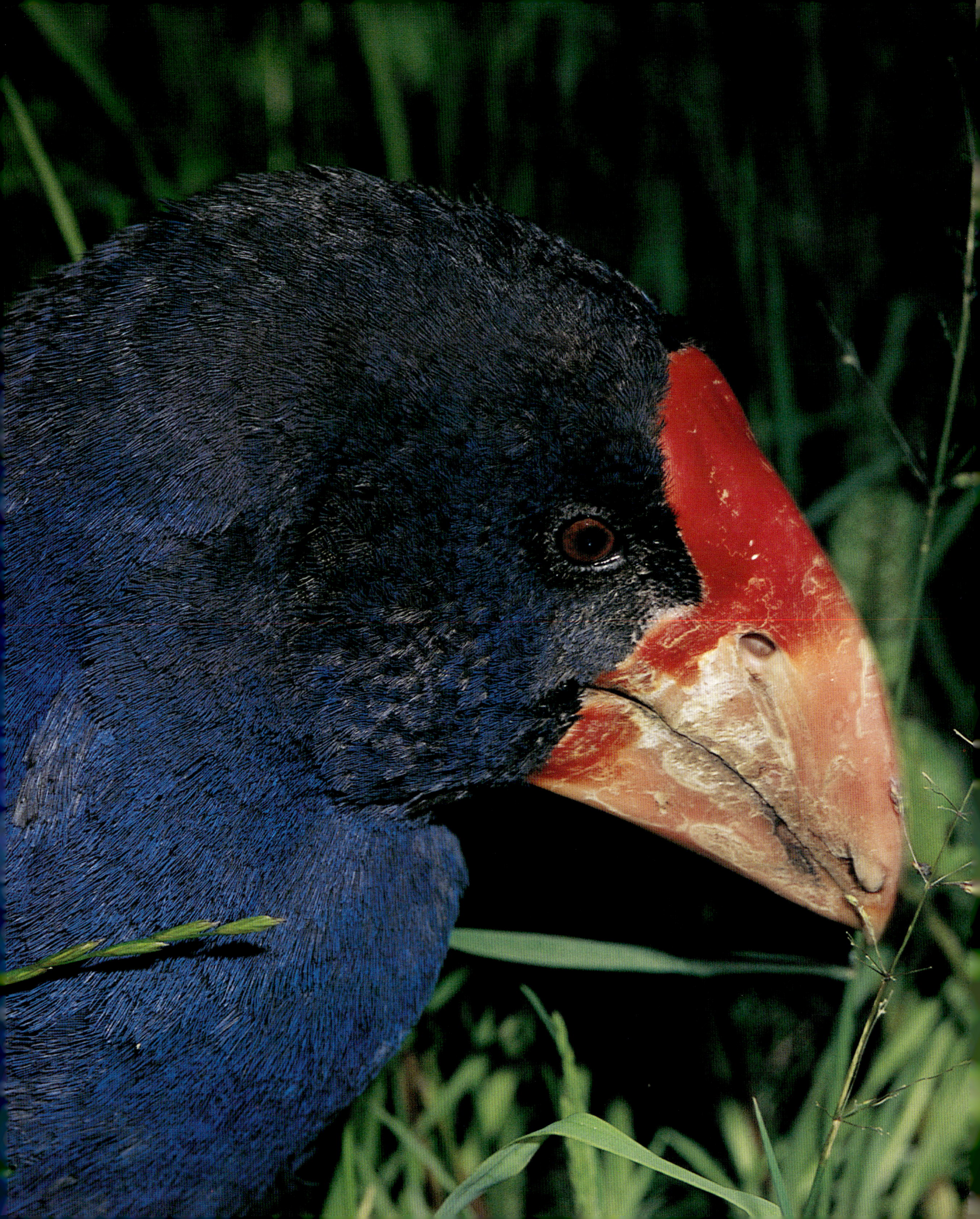

ate to compete for females during the breeding season. In the case of the kakapo, males construct a complex of tracks and bowls. At night the male booms, an extraordinary low frequency sound which can carry up to five kilometres. According to Butler (1989), males have been recorded making up to a thousand booms an hour and on one occasion this continued for 17 hours without a break. Little wonder that they lose weight during the breeding season.

There may be no kakapo left in Fiordland now, except perhaps for an isolated male or two. Most of the remaining 50 or so birds are protected on predator-free offshore islands further north, and under the control of breeding programmes run by the Department of Conservation. Unfortunately, the kakapo is a reluctant breeder, apparently breeding only after mast years, which are years when podocarp trees fruit *en masse*. This provides the kakapo with a higher than normal protein intake, as well as an abundance of sugars which give energy.

In 1849, Walter Mantell caught a live takahe in Dusky Bay. Long known to Maori, takahe were an occasional contributor to their middens. Mantell's find was the first live specimen brought to the attention of western science. The scientific name *Notornis mantelli* honours Mantell, who also unearthed the first takahe bones in North Island moa beds. His father, Dr Gideon Mantell, read the account of this capture to the Zoological Society in London in 1850. The bird was captured by sealers:

"upon being captured [it] uttered loud screams, and fought and struggled violently; it was kept alive three or four days on board the schooner and then killed, and the body roasted and ate by the crew, each partaking of the dainty, which was declared to be delicious."

Further takahe proved elusive and only four more specimens came to scientific attention during the next century. In 1948, however, Dr Geoffrey Orbell laid to rest what was practically an obsession for him, by finally locating a live takahe in what he named Takahe Valley.

The population, estimated at several hundred birds, underwent a decline in the 1970s, perhaps as a result of competition from deer. Takahe eat tussock stalks, nipping off the tips and discarding the rest. This allows regeneration of the plant, but deer eat the tops, damaging the tussock. Culling of deer did not solve the problem; neither did attempts to improve tussocks by topdressing with fertiliser. Fortunately, takahe are relatively easy to rear. A Department of Conservation recovery programme is centred on a chick-rearing unit at Te Anau.

Kakapo and takahe are the most extreme examples of threatened Fiordland bird life, but the problem was identified a century ago. The pioneering conservationist Richard Henry wrote in 1903:

(Above) **Competition with deer for food and predation by rats, cats and stoats means survival of the takahe depends on captive breeding programmes.**

(Left) **The takahe *Notornis mantelli*, once thought to be extinct, was rediscovered by Dr Geoffrey Orbell in 1948 in a remote Fiordland valley. This was the first known sighting in 50 years.**

…just now the "lords of creation" have imported ferrets and weasels that prey on all such things that sleep on the ground, and as kakapos cannot be expected to learn in a day what their race had forgotten for thousands of years, the chapter of their history is in all likelihood coming to a close. Fortunately they have many friends, and the New Zealand government takes a kindly interest in their affairs, and has appointed two reserves and men to put them out upon islands.

Richard Henry recognised the problems faced by New Zealand's native birds and he laboured long and hard to do something about it. Over a period of six years he located and captured around 400 kakapo and kiwi. Henry ferried these to the predator-free Resolution Island where he thought they would be safe. On 28 August 1900, his world collapsed around him: "I am very sorry to have to say that I saw a stoat on Resolution."

Predator-free islands are hard to establish and maintain. In the mid-1980s, the Department of Conservation eliminated rats from Breaksea Island with a controlled poisoning programme. They honed their technique on the smaller Hawea Island, utilising poison bait inside plastic tubes. The baits were set over a 40-metre grid and were checked and replaced daily. Twelve days after poisoning started, no further baits were taken. In late May 1986 Hawea was declared rat-free.

Wairaki Island shows us what the Fiordland coastline may have been like before we altered it forever. Here, amongst other offshore islands, there is a population of the endemic Fiordland skink *Leiolopisma acrinasum*,

(Below) **Richard Henry on Resolution Island; Moss-covered remains of Henry's kakapo pen on Pigeon Island, Dusky Sound.**

(Right) **Kakapo *Strigops habroptilus* were once common in Fiordland. Introduced predators such as stoats, rats and cats had a devastating impact. The last known Fiordland bird was transferred to an offshore island sanctuary in the 1980s to join the remaining 50 or so kakapo in existence at the time.**

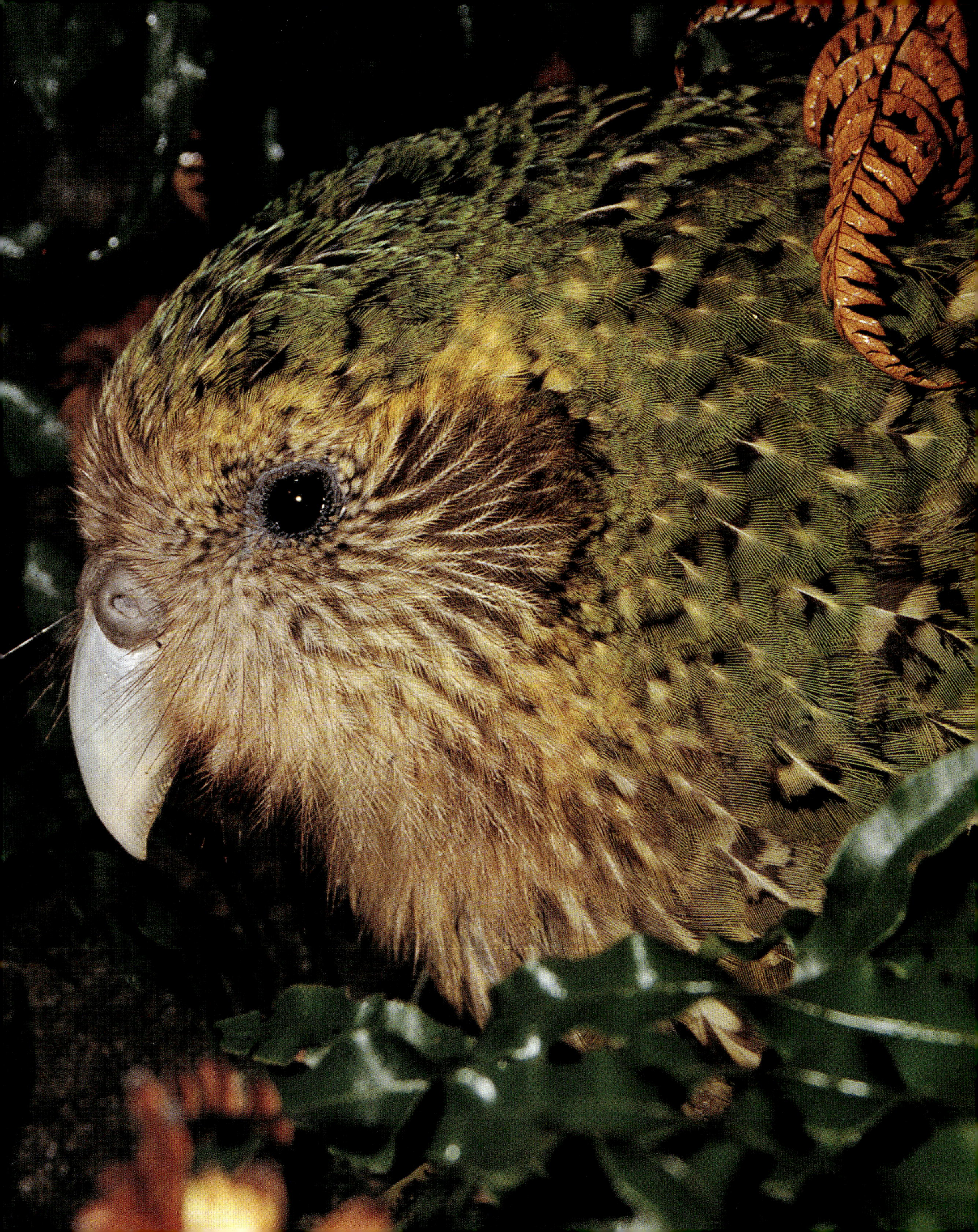

possibly the southernmost lizard in the world. These almost black lizards once lived in enormous numbers on the mainland. On summer days rock faces come alive with them as they scuttle back and forth after food. Their diet is primarily small invertebrates. Their black coloration is probably an adaptation to the rigour of the southern climate. It absorbs heat rapidly and enables these engaging lizards to reach operating temperature quickly. The presence of seals and seabirds probably helps. In the almost complete absence of vegetation their droppings provide the basis of a short and simple food chain. Some observers have reported seeing Fiordland skinks diving into pools. Fiordland skinks usually give birth to two young, in January or February.

Giant knobbled weevils *Hadramphus stilbocarpae* live on some of the rat-free islands of Breaksea Sound and on Five Fingers Peninsula of Resolution Island. Where they are found elsewhere, the weevils feed on *Stilbocarpa lyalli*, a megaherb which may still be found in parts of Fiordland. In Fiordland the weevils live on *Anistome lyalli*; so specialised are they that the larvae feed upon the roots while adults feed on the sap. Adults hide during the day and make concerted attacks on individual plants, which may die as a result. These feeding congregations may make the knobbled weevil vulnerable to rats. Meads (1990) states that the presence or absence of the knobbled weevil is a good indicator of the presence or absence of rats on an island.

Probably the most spectacular of Fiordland's insects is the batwinged cannibal fly *Exul singularis*, models of which can be seen on the wall of the boat terminal at Milford. The batwinged cannibal fly was first observed in Milford in 1901 and again at the entrance to the Homer Tunnel in 1989. They use their large black wings to soak up heat and when warm enough catch flying insects from which they suck the juices. No larvae have ever been found and nothing is known about its life history. According to Meads (1990) it is regarded as the world's rarest fly. However, more recently its habitat has been more precisely defined by the Otago Museum and it can no longer be considered as so rare.

The most annoying insect in Fiordland is the sandfly, also known as the blackfly *Austrosimulium* spp. The females require a blood meal for the eggs to develop properly and they are not too choosy over the source. Seals, birds or humans – it's all the same to the sandfly. You may be driven near to insanity by the attentions of sandflies. If you are a diver you will find that they will unerringly home in on the only pieces of bared flesh. They are at their worst when you are perched precariously on one leg while trying frantically to pull your wetsuit up the other. They thrive in Fiordland because the larvae live in running freshwater, a commodity Fiordland has in abundance.

Sandflies are one component of the Fiordland fauna which has changed little since Cook's day. In 1773 he wrote that sandflies were:

...exceedingly numerous and are so troublesome that they exceed everything of the kind I ever met with, wherever they light they cause a swelling and such an intolerable itching that it is not possible to refrain from scratching and at last ends in ulcers like the small Pox.

Robert Paulin was also lacking in enthusiasm in 1889:

We landed once or twice, but found the sandflies so savage that we were glad to take to our boat again.

160 FIORDLAND UNDERWATER

(Left) **The kea *Nestor notabilis* is a large, aggressive bird that nests in high alpine areas of the South Island and survived the onslaught of mammalian predators better than most others.**

(Opposite page) **Sandflies *Austrosimulium* spp. feed on the blood of any available vertebrate.**

These pests were apparently not in anyway put about by a downpour which one would have imagined quite capable of washing them all away. They seemed, in fact, to move slowly about among the thick rain drops without being touched by them.

But you don't need anecdotal evidence about the savagery of Fiordland's sandflies, you can sample them yourself by leaving your repellent off.

The topside community is in a state of flux as introduced species continue to move into the more remote areas of the park. In time, barring further catastrophic mammalian introductions, a new equilibrium will occur.

Much as it is regretted that the pristine terrestrial environment has gone, it still contributes to and moulds the character of the waters in the fiords. Extreme vigilance is required to ensure that the marine realm is not similarly threatened by any accidental introductions of marine organisms.

(Right) **Sandfly populations are high in Fiordland because the fresh running water habitat required by the larvae is freely available.**

The Life-cycle of Te Namu, the Sandfly

1. A sandfly's life begins with a raft of yellow-orange eggs laid on rocks or plants under the surface of a swift stream.
2. From the mouth, two fine-haired brushes strain food particles from the water, passing them to the mouth.
3. Should the larva wish to move, a patch of silk is laid down in preparation for the next manoeuvre.
4. Using a hook-fringed false leg near the head, the animal loops the loop to its new location.
5. At other times the larva goes fishing, letting itself into the current on the end of a silken thread.
6. When the larva is ready to pupate, it builds a small cone-shaped case.
7. After pupation the newly-emerged sandfly rides in a bubble of air to the water surface. Its wings expand and harden as it begins to fly. The process from egg to adulthood takes about seven weeks.

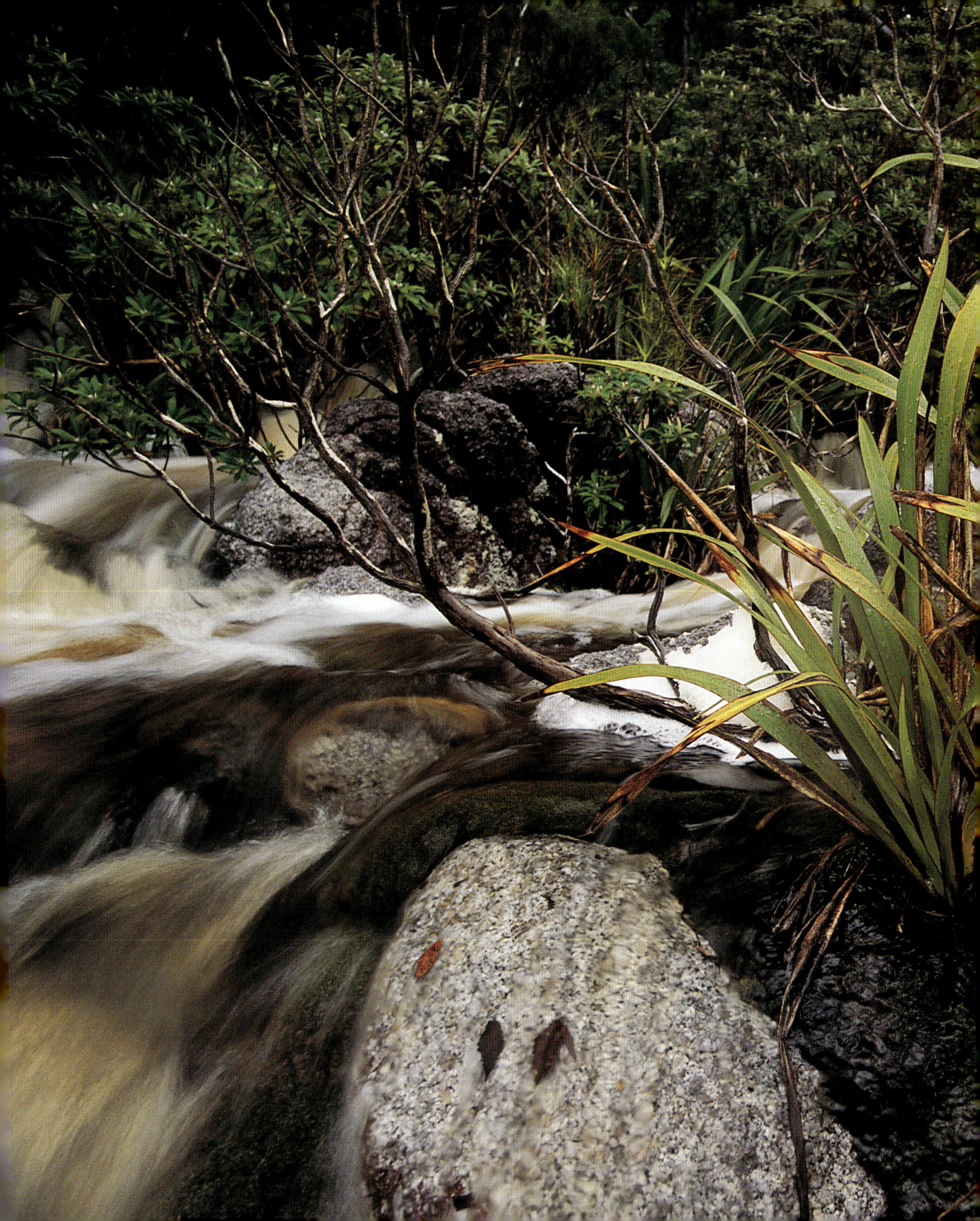

16

Research

JAMES Cook in the *Endeavour* was the first known European to record sighting the Fiordland coast in 1770. He returned on the *Resolution* in 1773 and spent six weeks in Dusky Sound. It was during this time that the naturalists on board recorded and described many New Zealand marine (and terrestrial) organisms for the first time. Johann and George Forster collected and painted numerous plants and animals. Unfortunately as a result of disagreements with the British Admiralty, their work was not published. Some of the manuscripts were consulted by other naturalists of the day, and many of their fish descriptions were published over 70 years later in Germany. It was not until the 200th anniversary of Cook's first expedition that several of the paintings were published (Whitehead 1968), but many still remain unpublished.

In the 1850s naval surveying of Fiordland began in detail by Captain Stokes on the *Acheron* and these surveys formed the basis of all naval charts for the region until the 1990s, when a new survey was at last carried out. Prospectors and surveyors from the newly established Geological Survey explored the fiords and studied the geological history. Dredging carried out as part of the geological work brought strange new organisms to the surface – the sea pen *Sarcophyllum bollonsi* was described by Benham in 1906 and the first record of a featherstar in New Zealand was *Comanthus benhami* described from Preservation Inlet in 1916.

After the 1940s marine biologists began to investigate the organisms of Fiordland in more detail. Extensive collections of molluscs and echinoderms were described by Fleming 1948 and 1950, Fell 1952 and Dell 1956.

Ecological studies dominated the 1960s and the New Zealand Oceanographic Institute carried out multi-disciplinary studies which covered hydrology, physical oceanography, sedimentology, geology, microbiology, diatoms, foraminifera, pollen, echinoderms, molluscs, brachiopods, and benthic ecology (Skerman 1964, Glasby 1978).

A series of bathymetric charts was produced between 1960 and 1985. Ecological studies of the intertidal communities and the deep muddy fiord bottoms followed (Batham 1965, McKnight 1968, 1969). These studies found that the organisms present were similar to those elsewhere in New Zealand but the fiord fauna

(Right) **Deep water emergence in the unique Fiordland ecosystem provides the opportunity to study organisms otherwise inaccessible by scuba divers.**

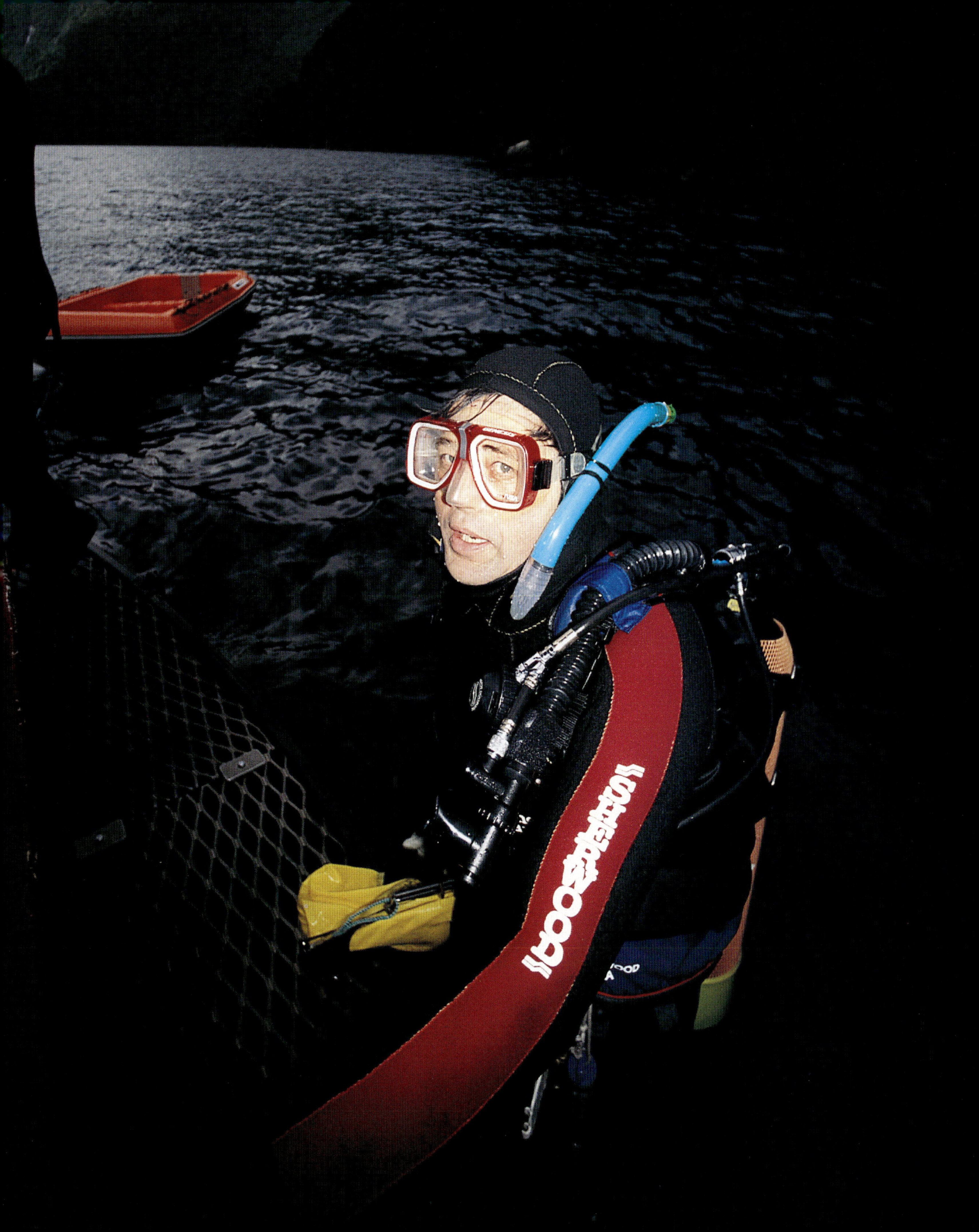
SHERWOOD

was impoverished, possibly because of the lowered salinities and lack of wave action in the intertidal.

In the 1970s, biologists began diving below the impoverished intertidal, carrying out scallop surveys for the commercial fishing industry. Other marine species were listed, including black coral, brachiopods, sponges, ascidians and bryozoans, but the unusual combination was not at first recognised as being significant. In the late 1970s attention focused on the steep rock walls and their unusual faunal assemblages. In a series of papers a unique and remarkable ecosystem was described: biological associations and physical oceanographic processes combining to produce a unique environment (see References).

It was soon realised that Fiordland is of immense value to marine scientists, enabling study of marine features in a near natural and undisturbed state, including populations of rare deep water organisms at diving depths, making it possible to carry out research that could not be done anywhere else in the world.

Many research projects are currently being carried out in Fiordland waters including studies of rock lobsters, fishes, kina, paua, brachiopods, black coral, sponge fauna and bioactive compounds, plankton communities, bacteria, deep basin faunas, rock wall ecology, physical oceanographic processes, suspended sediment, environmental parameters and geology by NIWA (National Institute of Water and Atmospheric Research); echinoderms, cetaceans, chemistry and organic compounds by the University of Otago; bioactivity by the University of Canterbury; biodiversity of fishes, algae, molluscs and crustaceans by the Museum of New Zealand; and seaweeds, kina, and conservation values by the Department of Conservation.

In addition, overseas institutions currently undertake a variety of joint projects with New Zealand scientists, including Florida International University – black coral; University of Pennsylvania – brachiopods; Northeastern University (Boston) – predation and recruitment; the Australian Institute of Marine Science – marine natural products; University of Exeter – crinoids; and the University of South Carolina – snakestars.

The near-pristine Fiordland environment also provides the opportunity to educate people at all levels about the organisms that inhabit the marine environment, the processes that operate there, and the need for careful management of these resources to ensure their sustainability. The educational hostel at Deep Cove, Doubtful Sound, is visited by over 3000 schoolchildren each year and represents an unrivalled facility for promotion of marine conservation to the next generation.

New Zealand has obligations to protect and preserve the marine environment under the Biodiversity Convention of the United Nations Convention on the Law of the Sea. The challenge for research in Fiordland, and New Zealand in general, is that because of the plethora of different pieces of legislation that affects the protection and use of marine resources, it is difficult to identify which organisations have overall accountability for the state of marine ecosystems and marine issues.

Research on marine biodiversity that urgently needs to be carried out to support appropriate policy and decision-making has not been identified for most sectors, and not in any integrated or comprehensive way. The baseline information is scarce and inadequate for assessing populations, risks to biodiversity and predicting, identifying and monitoring the effects of human-induced changes.

Conservationists are concerned that too much marine research is being dictated by fishing industry lobbyists who, because of property right issues under the Fisheries Management Regimes, exert inappropriate influence on the orientation of research (Nelson and Gordon, 1997). Research on the marine environment of Fiordland needs to be carried out in order that it can be inventoried, managed and protected by legislation, in perpetuity for all New Zealanders.

(Left) **Freshly collected 'deep water emergent' fishes, splendid perch and Fiordland brotula, being prepared prior to immersion in formalin on board research vessel in Preservation Inlet.**

(Right) **Scientists from Otago University and NIWA drilling holes in the fiord wall during coral transplant experiments.**

(Below) **Sorting specimens for preservation in the national collection at the Museum of New Zealand.**

(Opposite page) **Before the development of scuba, the underwater wilderness of Fiordland was unknown.**

168 FIORDLAND UNDERWATER

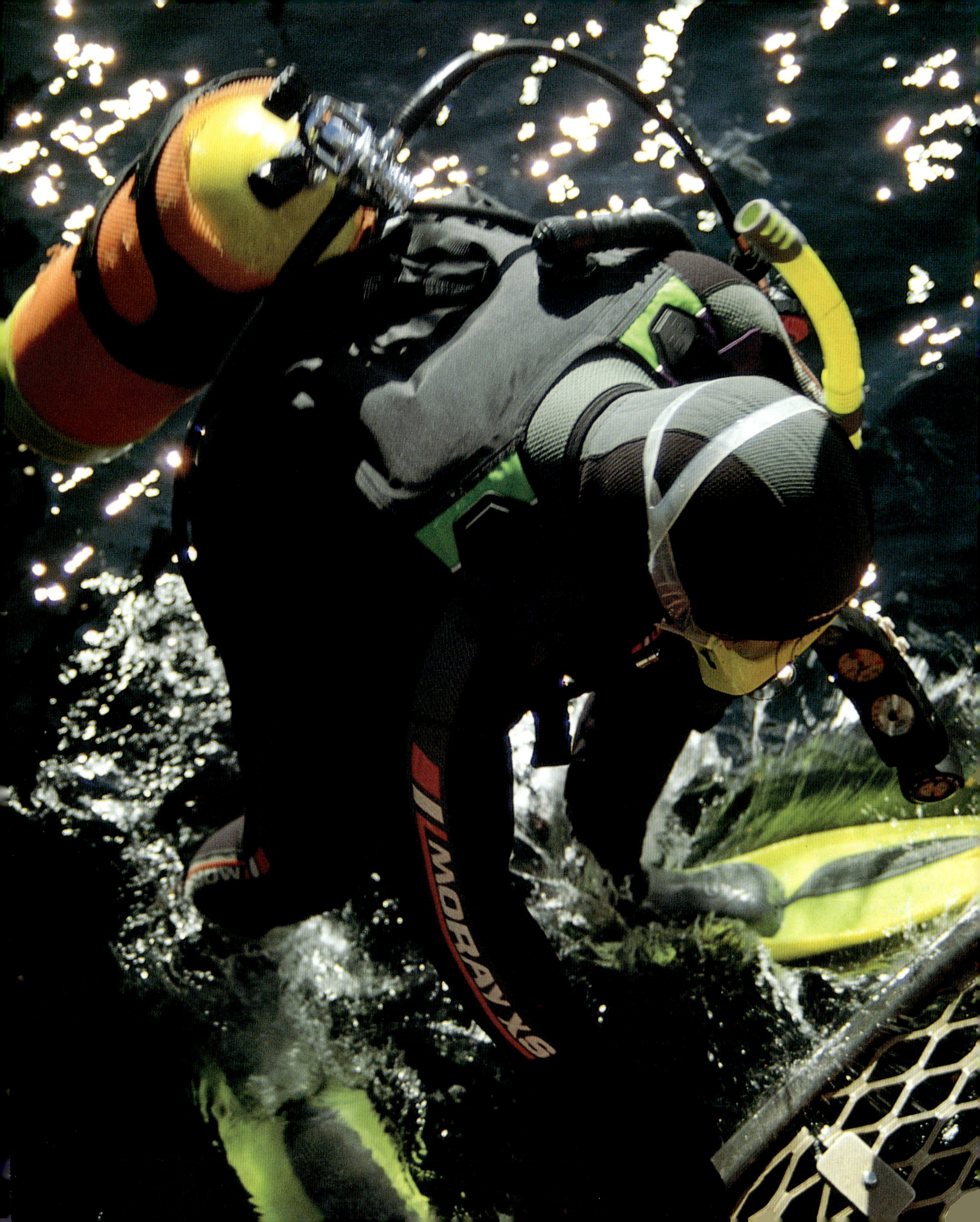
MORAY XS

17

Human Impact

ALTHOUGH Fiordland was one of the first places in New Zealand to be settled by Europeans, for an unknown number of years before that, Maori groups had made the long trip to collect Bowenite, the soft green rock known to them as *tangiwai*. It was also a valuable place for collecting food. Early European whalers and sealers were soon followed by fishermen, prospectors, miners and sawmillers, and later by hunters, recreational anglers and tourists. More recently, utilisation of the area has increased, in line with government policies where conservation is associated with the economics of the worldwide growth of 'ecotourism' rather than environmental protection.

Fiordland is part of the traditional mana whenua of Ngai tahu whanui and modern Ngai tahu Maori involvement in the fishing industry can be traced back through whakapapa lines into the ancient times.

Some of the earliest recorded comments by Europeans on New Zealand fisheries resources and Maori use of those resources are found in the journals of Captain James Cook and members of his crew, and were made during the visit of the *Resolution* to Dusky Sound in April-May 1773.

The southern Maori harvested and utilised a wide range of fish and shellfish resources. The mahinga kai were widespread and numerous, and were controlled at a hapu (family) or whanau (village) level. Today, the Ngai tahu whanui claim rights to all of the southern fisheries. Those rights were never disposed of and are guaranteed to them under the Treaty of Waitangi. The Maori Fisheries Act 1989 and the Treaty of Waitangi Settlement Act 1992 recognise those rights and allow for the establishment of Taiapure or Mataitai as a means acceptable to both Treaty partners for management of the resource, meeting the changing demands of the modern world and the requirements of the Act.

Commercial fishing in Fiordland began with sealing in 1792, but by the 1820s the seal population was reduced to a level where sealing was no longer economic. Whaling in the area suffered a similar fate. A whaling station was established in Preservation Inlet in 1829, but the venture lasted less than 10 years. Today the fiords support highly valued commercial recreational and charter boat fishing, principally targeting rock lobster (crayfish), paua, and blue cod.

(Right) **The Department of Conservation vessel *Renown* provides support for research and enables monitoring of coastal activities.**

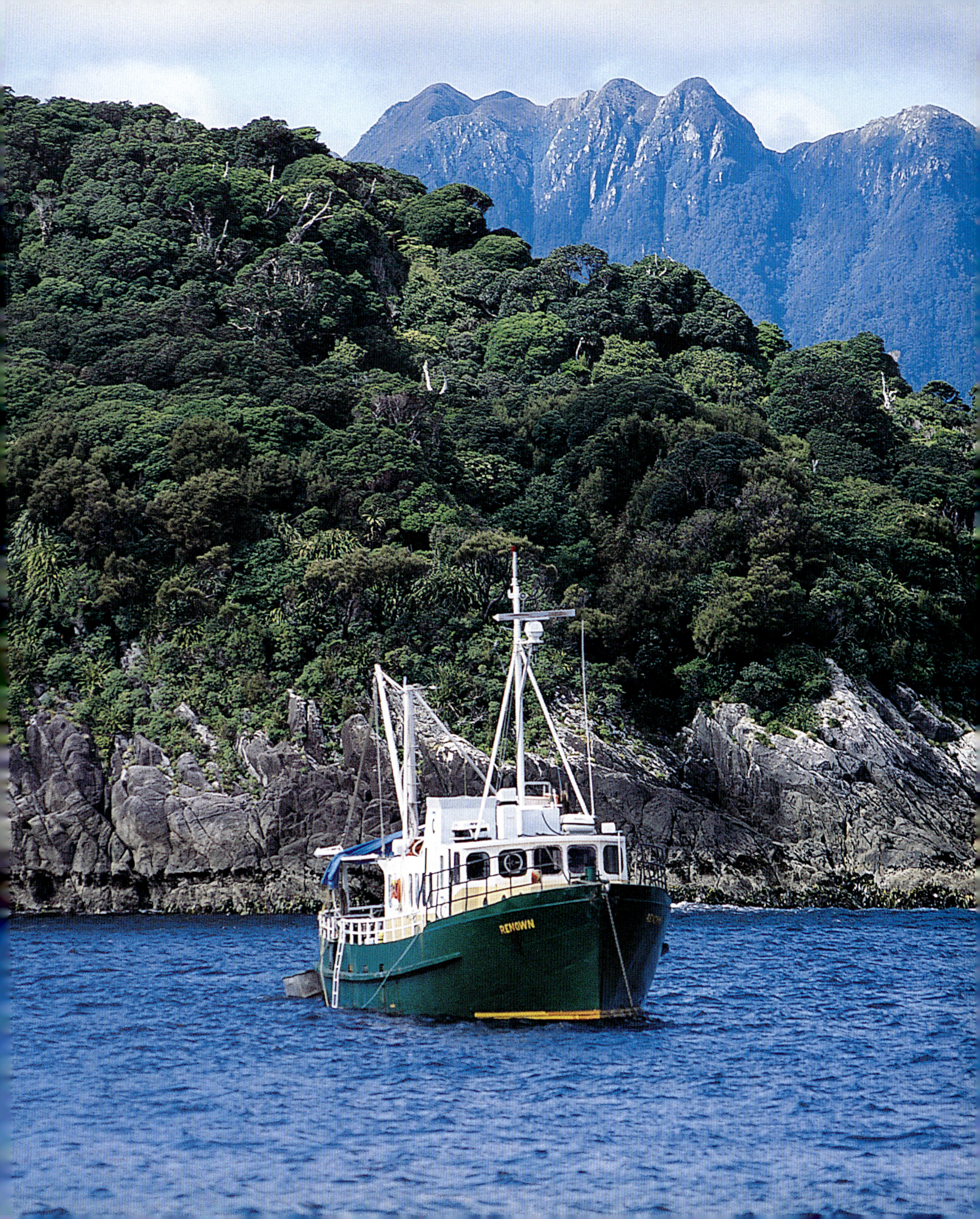
RENOWN

The early blue cod fishery consisted of line fishing from dinghies, based in the fishing village at North Port, Chalky Inlet, until the fishery closed down at the outbreak of World War II. After the war, a combination of new technological developments (especially refrigeration) and the opening up of the American market for rock lobster tails sparked the beginning of the commercial rock lobster fishery.

The distance from markets, and the unbroken mountain chain of the Southern Alps formed a formidable barrier, effectively isolating Fiordland except for road access via the Homer Tunnel to Milford Sound (from the 1950s), and over the Wilmot Pass to Doubtful Sound (from the early 1970s). Limited access to Fiordland had always been available from Bluff to those with suitably sized vessels. However, a notorious weather pattern of persistent westerly gales (Puysegur Point on the southwestern tip of Fiordland is the windiest place in New Zealand) had presented major problems with the transfer of catch from fishing vessel to processing factory.

In the past, fish tended to be kept on board the fishing vessel for periods of four to six weeks, or even longer. Economics, namely the unacceptable risk of holding large quantities of fish on board, should the vessel be lost (as too frequently happened) changed this trend. Bringing the catch to port in favourable weather often resulted in enforced confinement when adverse weather prevented a return to the fiords.

The introduction of aircraft to transport supplies in and freight high-value rock lobster tails out to Te Anau or Invercargill by floatplane or helicopter revolutionised the industry. Fishing activity increased dramatically, but not without cost: more than 70 fishing vessels were lost in a 10-year period and in the early 1980s, a Ministry of Agriculture and Fisheries report concluded that the rock lobster fishery survived only by the grace of the greatest conservation factor of all, the weather.

Some finfish, mainly groper, blue cod and shark, are caught outside the fiords but the main species fished commercially in this area are crayfish and paua. The total Fiordland rock lobster harvest, in excess of 800 tonnes per annum, is roughly one-third of the national catch, and similar to catches in the 1950s, despite the greater number of boats today. Anecdotal comments by older fishermen suggest that there are fewer rock lobster available; however, annual population fluctuations are large and obscure any trends.

With the liberalisation of paua export provisions during the 1980s, commercial harvesting of paua in Fiordland became economic. In 1998 the Fiordland Total Allowable Catch for paua was 147 tonnes (12 percent of the national harvest per annum). McShane (1994) found evidence for localised recruitment failure in paua stocks in some areas.

Commercial species, such as rock lobster, paua and blue cod, are protected and conserved by the Ministry of Fisheries Quota Management System (QMS) which was introduced in 1986 and ensures fish stocks remain sustainable by controlling the harvest. The QMS also introduced tradeable property rights into the fishery. Additional regulatory controls to ensure sustainability of the stocks include such measures as escape gaps on lobster pots, minimum legal takeable sizes and a ban on the use of scuba in the paua fishery.

Although no protection is available for other non-commercial species (with the exception of black and red corals), regulations aimed at protecting the Fiordland habitat include prohibition of trawling and other bulk harvesting methods. The 1996 Fisheries Act strengthened provisions relating to safeguarding the marine environment.

The resident community in Fiordland have long utilised the fiords for recreational fishing and more recently, recreational fishing enthusiasts from throughout New Zealand have been taking advantage of the charter operations available. Recreational collecting of scallops and crayfish, spear and line fishing is popular, particularly on the southern side of Milford and in Doubtful

(Left) Rock lobster fishing boat in heavy seas, outside Chalky Inlet. The greatest conservation factors in Fiordland are region's inaccessibility and the weather.

(Lower) Derelict vessels are used in several fiords to provide storage facilities where the topography is too steep to land.

HUMAN IMPACT *173*

Sound, which are the principle access points to the fiords. Milford Sound has been closed to commercial fishing by the Southland and Sub-Antarctic Areas Commercial Fishing Regulations 1986 and the northern side of Milford Sound and The Gut in Doubtful Sound were gazetted as marine reserves in 1993.

Boats and vehicles are transported over Lake Manapouri by barge, giving access to Doubtful, Thompson and Bradshaw Sounds via Wilmot Pass. The use of Dusky and George Sounds for recreational fishing and diving for crayfish is increasing. Recreational fishing methods are almost exclusively either line fishing or hand gathering while diving and are restricted to the fiords closest to the points of access, unlike commercial and tourist operations which take place throughout the whole of Fiordland. However, changes in access indicate that there is potential for expansion of the recreational catch.

Recreational fishing is controlled by daily bag limits for each angler, although there is no limit on the number of anglers and, until the 1990s, no record of the recreational catch. Commercial fishermen, concerned that extraction rates remain sustainable and at acceptable levels, noted in their 1991 marine reserve proposal that recreational fishing is often difficult to control and overfishing on a localised basis can occur.

In the interests of maintaining a sustainable and managed fishery, Ngai tahu, with commercial, recreational, and charter boat representatives, formed the Guardians of Fiordland's Fisheries in 1995. Together with the Ministry of Fisheries, the Guardians are committed to sustainable utilisation of the finite fishery resources of Fiordland, and have begun the painstaking task of gathering data on current catch rates and identifying information gaps and research needs.

The involvement of the Guardians, who collectively have a wealth of knowledge and experience, in the decision-making process will enable a cautious and responsible approach to developing new fisheries and ensure the current level of fish stocks is maintained or improved. Education is also one of the most important functions of the Guardians and as a consequence they have advocated for research projects to be carried out and have developed a code of fishing practices.

Fiordland has an environment designated as a 'World Heritage Park', attracting many visitors (estimated in 1997 at 450,000 per year). In addition to the terrestrial features and the coastline, the underwater features are spectacular, as this book illustrates. At present the remoteness of the fiords somewhat limits the number of visitors but the potential of tourism to increase rapidly is a factor that must be carefully considered.

The number of charter boat operators, ranging from sea kayaks to tourist launches, is estimated at 20 to 30 and is increasing, providing employment for more people in the region. The area is visited by large cruise vessels like the *Royal Viking Star*, *Souka*, and *Marco Polo*. These vessels regularly visit Dusky, Doubtful, Thompson and Milford Sounds and current estimates suggest around 20 to 25 vessels make 40 visits per year (N.Z. Customs *pers. comm*).

Worldwide shortages of freshwater will bring increasing pressure to revisit proposals to export water from Deep Cove using large tankers. No environmental impact assessment of the effects of these large vessels has been carried out. Impacts could arise from wash-generated waves, propeller wake mixing surface freshwater with the deeper salt water and discharge of ballast water and sewage. Under the Southland Regional Coastal Plan, all New Zealand registered vessels are prohibited from discharging ballast water within the coastal marine area, and human sewage within two nautical miles of land.

Non-extractive ecotourism will also increase pressure on the marine environment through sewage disposal, rubbish removal and the number of anchorages or moorings required. While the extraordinary underwater

(Right) **Mitre Peak provides an imposing backdrop to the Milford Underwater Observatory at Harrison Cove, where non-divers can experience the underwater world of the fiords.**

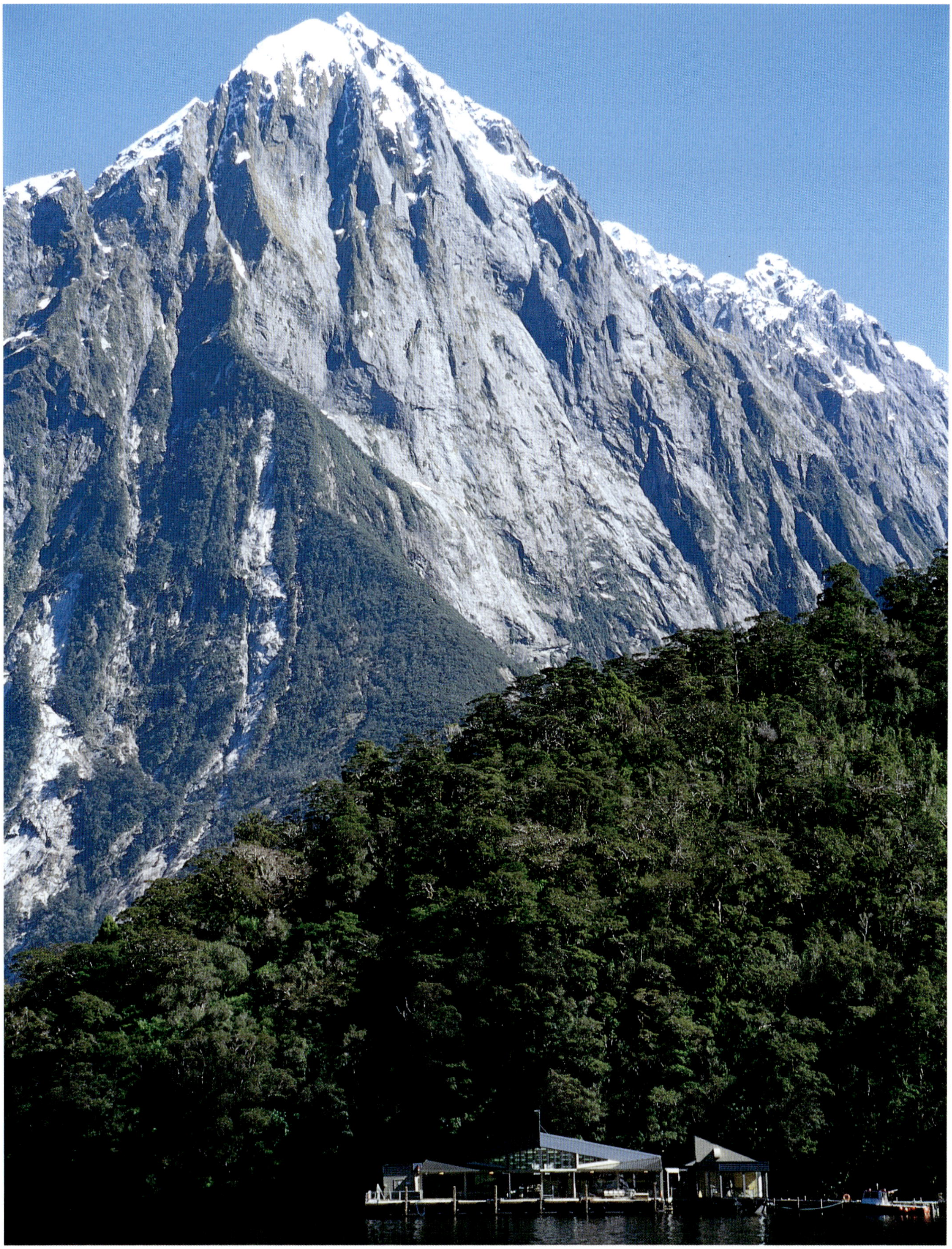

(Right) **Milford Underwater Observatory** is an educational facility offering visitors an insight into Fiordland below the waterline.

(Lower) **Fiord organisms** can be viewed by visitors through underwater windows at the Observatory.

176 FIORDLAND UNDERWATER

scenery appears to be the primary reason for the increasing numbers of divers visiting the region, many also gather crayfish or spear fish. No figures are yet available on the types or levels of activity undertaken by divers.

Because of the sheltered nature of the fiords, the corals and bryozoans on the fiord walls are extremely fragile and susceptible to damage by divers, not only through direct contact but also through water movement created by fins. Divers in Fiordland have to be skilled in bouyancy control. Unlike other areas where divers can rest on clear areas of seafloor, the vertical fiord walls require them to remain suspended in midwater. Uncontrolled 'bouncing' off any rock ledges or the cliff-face itself can destroy many delicate sessile invertebrates which may have taken decades to grow.

Recreational diving may need to be restricted to designated areas and monitored as a means of studying the effects of direct and indirect damage. Wholesale banning of diving activities in Milford Sound has been proposed, although the rationale for this seems to be based on congestion and navigation of tour boats rather than conservation.

There have been few studies of the effects of tour boats on dolphins, although research indicates changes in dolphin behaviour when boats are present. Concerns are that dolphins may be encouraged to leave the area, or that boats may interfere with important behaviours like foraging and breeding. Next to nothing is known about any long-term effects of tour boats on survival or reproductive success of dolphins, and so far it has only been possible to document immediate changes in behaviour and physical damage from propellers and boat collisions. However, there may be educational advantages and long-term benefits as a result of dolphin encounters, with visitors gaining knowledge or changing their behaviour with respect to marine mammals in particular or the environment in general.

Everyone who visits Milford Sound can now get a revealing glimpse of the hidden wilderness. The Milford Underwater Observatory was opened in December 1995. Situated in Harrison Cove just a short boat ride from Milford Village, it consists of a reception area with a variety of interpretative displays that explain the uniqueness and fragility of the Fiordland environment, and an underwater viewing platform that looks out onto specially-constructed and stocked trays holding examples of Fiordland fauna. These are the immobile animals, the corals, the tube anemones, the horse mussels, the tubeworms and hosts of others. The presence of the mobile creatures depends upon the attractiveness of the trays and the quality of their maintenance.

The Observatory is an excellent educational facility, providing the visitor with a fuller understanding of the delicate natural treasures concealed beneath the dark waters of this remote and wild region.

The residents and users of Fiordland have long recognised the fragility of the ecosystem here. Today this is threatened by the ease of access for the visitor who can penetrate the remotest fiords then leave, often within a few hours. The impact of these brief visits may not be realised by the visitor and the effect each individual has may not be significant in itself, but long-term, the consequences may be disastrous for the region if access is left uncontrolled.

Milford Sound has for some years been one of New Zealand's most popular visitor destinations, with up to 2500 visitors a day, of whom a large proportion travel by coach from Queenstown and Te Anau. The remoteness and large area covered by the Fiordland National Park ensures that complete enforcement of restrictive activities is virtually impossible; however, the limited road access via Milford or Doubtful Sounds enables relatively easy monitoring of land access and extraction.

Protection and enhancement of the area for *all* users is the responsibility of those same users. This requires an appropriate and acceptable management framework founded on comprehensive local knowledge, sound academic research, and supported by legislation.

18

Environmental Management

MANAGEMENT of the New Zealand coastal zone is carried out by Regional Councils under the Resource Management Act 1991, while conservation and fisheries management are the responsibilities of the Department of Conservation and Ministry of Fisheries respectively.

The Regional Coastal Plan, which includes the Fiordland region, is prepared by the Southland Regional Council, for approval by the Minister of Conservation. Standing alongside the Department of Conservation is the New Zealand Conservation Authority, a national citizen body charged with providing advice to the Minister of Conservation, approving conservation management strategies and investigating conservation matters of national importance. Coastal management is therefore, in theory at least, based on a partnership between the local community and the Crown.

Management of the Fiordland coastal region is undertaken at three levels:

1. The New Zealand Coastal Policy Statement (1993) prepared by the Minister of Conservation, which sets out the broad framework for management of the coastal environment;
2. The Regional Policy Statement, which takes into account the matters within the New Zealand Coastal Policy Statement and provides the specific policy framework for the management of the coastal zone within the Southland region;
3. The Regional Coastal Plan, prepared by the Southland Regional Council and approved by the Minister of Conservation, details the methods and procedures to manage the coastal environment.

The Fiordland terrestrial environment is protected under the National Parks Act 1980; however, this protection stops at high tide (mean high water spring) and the fiord marine environment is excluded from both the Fiordland National Park and the South West New Zealand Te Wahipounamu World Heritage Area.

In 1990, when Fiordland National Park was included in the World Heritage Area, the UNESCO World Heritage Committee noted the importance of including the waters of the fiords as an integral part of this national park. They welcomed the initiatives of the New Zealand

(Right) **Humic acids dissolved from vegetation by the high rainfall stain stream water, which flows into the fiords to form a surface layer responsible for the unique marine environment of Fiordland.**

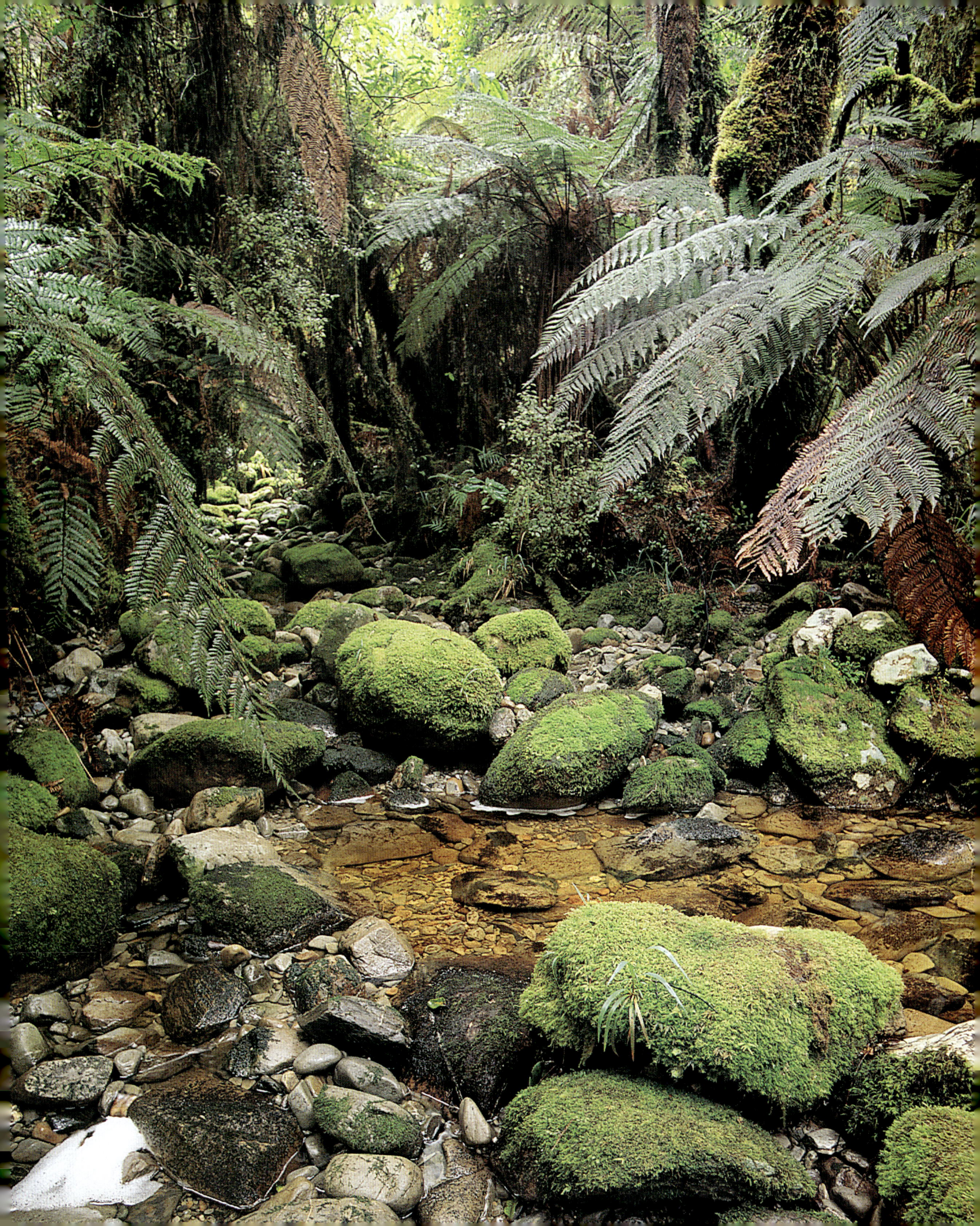

authorities to bring the waters of the fiords under the control of the Park.

An Environmental Impact Audit by the Commission for the Environment in July 1984, on a proposal to export water from Deep Cove by Triune Resources Corporation, recommended that:

> The Ministers of Lands and Transport take all necessary steps to ensure that semi-enclosed coastal waters within National Parks, such as the fiords, have reserve status compatible with that of the surrounding land area.

In 1986, concerns were expressed by divers over the problems of rubbish disposal in some areas of Fiordland and the lack of protection of the marine environment (*New Zealand Dive Magazine* Vol 8, No. 4).

In November 1990, the Fiordland National Park Management Plan, approved by the New Zealand Conservation Authority, outlined an objective "to support the protection of the inshore marine waters adjoining the park." An appendix to the document outlined a proposal to consider the addition of the fiords to Fiordland National Park, but acknowledged that the National Parks Act 1980 does not provide for the inclusion of the sea or seabed within national parks, and the high waterline marks the boundary.

Since the 1980s an increase in awareness of the unique underwater environment has led to enlightened attitudes by fishermen and other commercial operators in Fiordland. In 1992 the Fiordland Fishermen's Association, the Fiordland Lobster Company and the New Zealand Commercial Fishermen's Association introduced a 'Voluntary Code of Practice' and proposed two marine reserves, one in Milford and one in Doubtful Sound (Olsen 1991). These marine reserves were gazetted on 1 November 1993. The southern side of Milford Sound is currently closed to commercial fishing but available for recreational fishing (Southland and Sub-Antarctic Areas Commercial Fishing Regulations 1986).

Grange (1990) outlined the need for greater protection within the fiords and identified seven areas for which protection was required. Anecdotal evidence suggests that damage to these areas has increased since the gazetting of the reserves has attracted divers.

Extending the marine reserves in Milford and Doubtful Sounds to all the fiords would provide protection and the value of the natural habitat would be maintained. Historically, marine reserves have been undervalued: a breach of the regulations attracted a maximum fine of only NZ$500. Amendments to the Marine Reserves Act have brought it into line with the Fisheries Act and penalties are now much more severe. However, the Ministry of Fisheries has no mandate to enforce regulations within a marine reserve, and the Department of Conservation is primarily a land management agency. The under-resourcing of DoC's marine responsibilities prevents effective monitoring and limits even basic educational activities such as adequate signage.

The exclusive nature of Marine Reserve Legislation is also incompatible with continued commercial and recreational fishing activities. Although the Marine Reserves Act provides the public freedom of access, a marine reserve can only be set aside for the purposes of preserving marine life, and harvest of seafood is not generally permitted. Often areas recognised as distinctive and worthy of preservation have long been used by various sectors of the public for recreational and commercial fishing. To protect a section of coast as a marine reserve, it must have the support of the public and of commercial fisheries. Furthermore, a marine reserve can only be established with the concurrence of the Minister of Fisheries and Transport.

The present representation of biodiversity in two Fiordland marine reserves is inadequate. The protected areas are too small: even with comprehensive research,

(Right) **Wetjacket Arm is situated off Acheron Passage between Breaksea and Dusky Sounds.**

(Previous page, Left) **The absence of browsing mammals from some isolated islands enables direct comparisons of the ecological impact of introduced animals on mainland vegetation.**

(Previous page, Right) **Stirling Falls, Milford Sound. Launches cater for thousands of tourists who visit this fiord on a daily basis, mainly in the summer months.**

management would be out of scale with the ecosystem. The ecosystem requires protection: commercial activities are integral parts of that ecosystem and must be taken into consideration. Establishing isolated small-scale protected areas, managing single-species fisheries, or totally protecting individual species for preservation can guard against human impact. However, protection of the ecosystem must be made at the broadest possible scale to enable decisions and actions to be incorporated into an overall management plan.

One possible approach to protection is that of the Biosphere Reserve. The Biosphere Reserve concept is a radical departure from many contemporary conservation approaches. It is part of the Man and the Biosphere Programme of UNESCO, and is based on the amazing concept that humans are an integral component of the system. A Biosphere Reserve links sustainable use with the normal functioning of the ecosystem involved, through aligning different agencies, mandates and statutes to promote effective and co-ordinated management – stewardship rather than control.

The Biosphere Reserve concept has been widely adopted internationally as a means of integrating conservation and development. Among its greatest assets is the emphasis given to co-ordinated application of research for solving resource management problems. In turn this promotes the development of long-term monitoring programmes aimed at revealing human impacts and reducing the ecological and social disruption. Despite considerable thought and investigation, no Biosphere Reserves have been established in New Zealand, primarily because their potential benefits for improving existing research, monitoring and management systems have not been adequately demonstrated.

An alternative to the Biosphere Reserve concept is the possibility of adding the marine environment to the existing South West New Zealand Te Wahipounamu World Heritage Area.

For a property to be included on the World Heritage List as natural heritage, the Committee must find it meets one or more of the following criteria:

1. Be outstanding examples representing the major stages of the earth's evolutionary history; or
2. Be outstanding examples representing significant ongoing geological processes, biological evolution and man's interaction with his natural environment. As distinct from the periods of the earth's development, this focuses upon ongoing processes in the development of plant and animal communities, landforms, and marine areas and freshwater bodies; or
3. Contain superlative natural phenomena, formations or features, for instance outstanding examples of the most important ecosystems, areas of exceptional natural beauty or exceptional combinations of natural and cultural elements; or
4. Contain the most important and significant natural habitats where threatened species of animals or plants of outstanding universal value, from the viewpoint of science or conservation, still survive.

Adding a property to the World Heritage list can produce many benefits as a result of greatly increased tourism. The potential revenue that can be generated from tourism may be far in excess of what may be derived by other uses which may threaten World Heritage values. However, without appropriate management, tourism itself is a threat to the fiord environment. In addition to increases in employment opportunities and income, local communities could also expect benefits from improved planning and management of the region, along with the availability of additional resources leading to improved facilities.

Inclusion of the marine environment of all the fiords in the South West New Zealand Te Wahipounamu World Heritage Area would provide greater recognition and protection for marine biodiversity in this globally unique environment and will produce many benefits. These include the recognition and protection of marine habitats

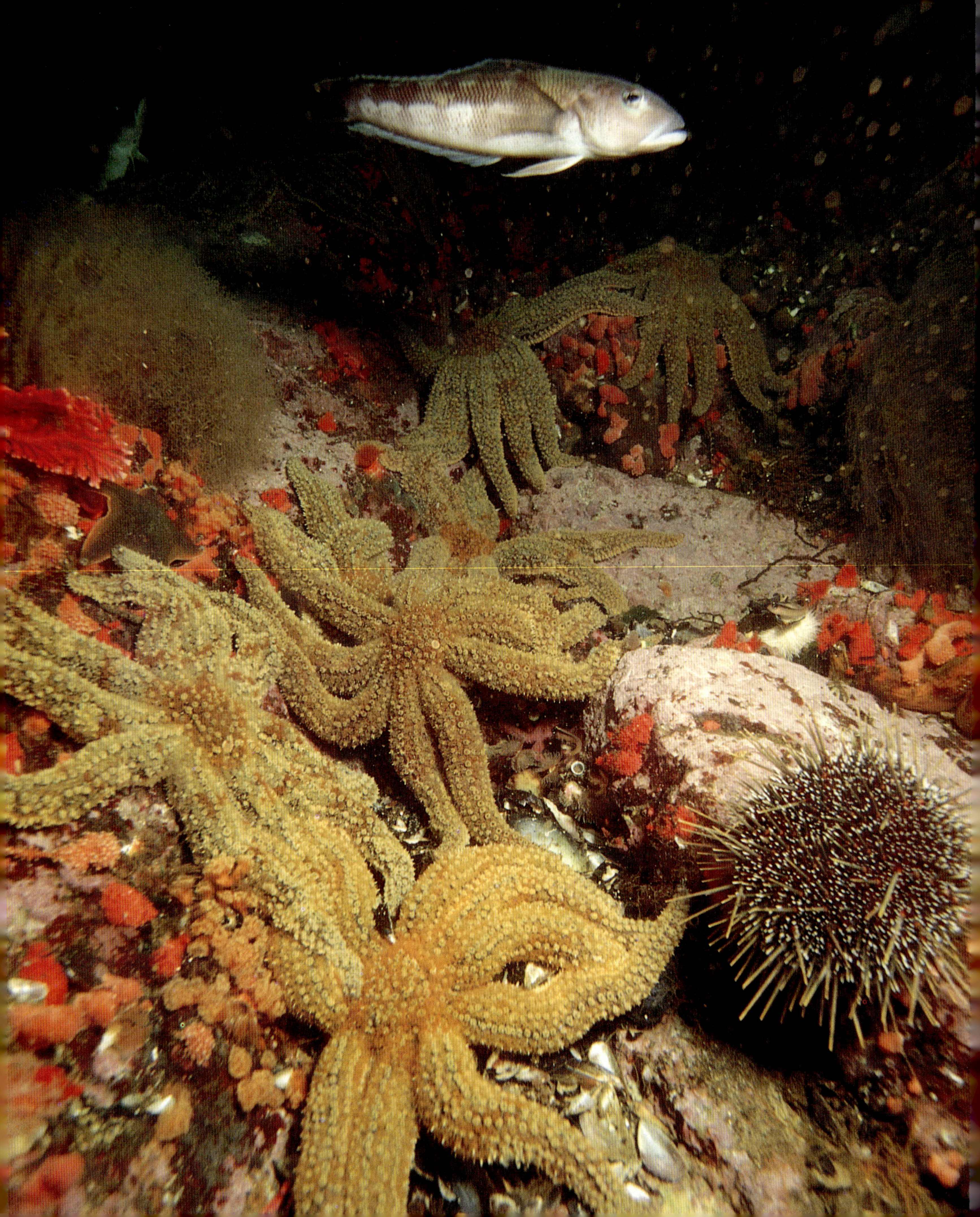

and organisms for their intrinsic worth, educational opportunities, new potentials for recreation and tourism, and encourage co-operation between governmental authorities and the private sector in developing methods for the sustainable use of biological resources.

New Zealand has an international obligation to protect and conserve World Heritage property. However, there is no impediment to existing uses unless they threaten the universal natural and cultural values of the property. Experience in overseas World Heritage sites shows that a wide range of activities can be undertaken and that local communities are not unduly inconvenienced. For example, on Lord Howe Island (inscribed as World Heritage property in 1982) residents carry out normal day-to-day community activities, while recreational and commercial fishing is undertaken on the Great Barrier Reef (inscribed 1981).

World Heritage listing does not affect ownership rights or control. Ownership remains as it was prior to nomination and state and local laws and regulations still apply. Ownership and control of World Heritage areas do not pass to any international body or foreign power. In New Zealand, management of World Heritage Areas is the responsibility of the Department of Conservation. Through the Conservation Authority this can be an effective partnership with local and national Maori, fishing, tourism and conservation groups, protecting Fiordland's unique marine environment while allowing sustainable use.

One hundred years after publication of Robert Paulin's book, public opinion led to the nomination of South West New Zealand Te Wahipounamu for inclusion in the World Heritage list in 1989. We believe that the Fiordland underwater environment is of equal importance to that of the terrestrial environment and meets all of the criteria for both Biosphere Reserve and World Heritage listing. The effusive sentiments expressed by Robert Paulin in 1889 probably reflect those of most visitors to Fiordland:

> ...and thus conclude my description of the West Coast Sounds of New Zealand:–
>
> A scene of stupendous beauty: I saw, as it were, silvered dome and mitred peak resting on darkness; through this darkness trailed a streak of silver, and down this silver trail we passed, on and on, under black cliffs that hung over us, like portals of eternal darkness, like the mouths of huge, endless, hellish caverns, breathing eternal gloom! – home of the spirit of night. And above this stupendous mass of obscurity float palaces of light, veils of luminous mist, pinnacles of topaz, lakes of pure white marble, and domes of fairy silver. It falls behind us, and we are out on the moon-silvered sea. The huge mountains sink and sink till they look like cloud-banks on the horizon. The southern swell moves silently past, making us stagger as we pace the deck. The land-wind strikes cold, and as the sounds are left behind, we turn in.

This book is dedicated to our children and to all the children of New Zealand. We hope that Fiordland's underwater realm will be protected long before our grandchildren experience the natural wonders of the hidden wilderness.

(Left) **Marine community immediately below the freshwater layer at the Strawberry Fields, Long Sound, Preservation Inlet.**

References

Begg, A.C. & Begg, N.C., 1966. *Dusky Bay*. Whitcombe & Tombs Ltd, Christchurch. 240 pp.

Begg, A.C. & Begg, N.C., 1973. *Port Preservation*. Whitcombe & Tombs Ltd, Christchurch. 398 pp.

Bell, J.D., Bell, S.M. & Tierney, L.D., 1992. MAF Fisheries South Region – Survey of Marine Recreational Fishers – Summary of Findings. New Zealand Fisheries Management Regional Series No. 1.

Bell, J.D., Bell, S.M. & Tierney, L.D., 1994. Results of the 1991-92 marine recreational fishing catch and effort survey. MAF Fisheries South Region – New Zealand Fisheries Data Report.

Bell, N. & Foster, P., (Eds), 1994. *A Boatie's Guide to Fiordland*. 2nd. Ed., Mana Cruising Club, Wellington. 113 pp.

Bennett, Q., 1986. Diving Fiordland. *New Zealand Dive Magazine* 8 (4): 4-6, 44-45.

Brailsford, B., 1984. *Greenstone Trails: the Maori Search for Pounamu*. Reed, Wellington. 192 pp.

Butler, D., 1989. *Quest for the Kakapo*. Heinemann Reed, Auckland. 136 pp.

Campbell, H.J. & Fleming, C.A., 1981. Brachiopods from Fiordland, New Zealand, collected during the New Golden Hind Expedition, 1946. *New Zealand Journal of Zoology* 8(2): 145-155.

Cobb, J., 1987. *Fiordland: The Incredible Wilderness*. Cobb/Horwood in association with the Department of Conservation, Auckland. 111 pp.

Department of Conservation, 1989. Nomination of South-West New Zealand (Te Wahipounamu) by the Government of New Zealand for inclusion in the World Heritage List. Department of Conservation, Wellington. 69 pp.

Department of Lands and Survey, 1986. *The Story of Fiordland National Park*. Published in association with Cobb/Horwood Publications, Auckland. 176 pp.

Duffy, C.A.J. & Ackley, J.C., 1988. *An Introduction to the Marine Invertebrates of the Kaikoura Region*. Laboratory Manual, University of Canterbury Zoology Department. 134 pp.

Fell, H.B., 1952. Echinoderms from southern New Zealand. Zoology Publications from Victoria University College, Wellington 18: 1-37.

Fleming, C.A., 1950. The molluscan fauna of the fiords of western Southland. *New Zealand Journal of Science and Technology* B35(5): 378-389.

Garner, D.M., 1964. The hydrology of Milford Sound. pp 25-33 in Skerman, T.M., (ed.), Studies of a southern Fiord. *New Zealand Oceanographic Institute Memoir 17*. 101pp.

Gaskin, D.E. 1972. *Whales, Dolphins and Seals*. Heinneman Educational Books, Auckland. 200 pp.

Given, D.R., 1981. *Rare and Endangered Plants of New Zealand*. A.H. & A.W. Reed, Wellington. 154 pp.

Glasby, G.P., (ed.), 1978. Fiord studies: Caswell and Nancy Sounds, New Zealand. *New Zealand Oceanographic Memoir 79*. 94 pp.

Grange, K.R., 1980. *Antipathes fiordensis*, a new species of black coral (Coelenterata: Antipatharia) from New Zealand. *New Zealand Journal of Zoology* 17: 279-282.

Grange, K.R., 1985. Distribution, standing crop, population structure and growth rates of black coral in the southern fiords of New Zealand. *New Zealand Journal of Marine and Freshwater Research* 19(4): 467-475.

Grange, K.R., 1988. Mutual protection in fiord waters. *Resource Research* 14: 1.

Grange, K.R., 1991. Mutualism between the antipatharian *Antipathes fiordensis* and the ophiuroid *Astrobranchion constrictum* in New Zealand fjords. *Hydrobiologia* 216/217: 297-303.

Grange, K.R., Singleton, R.J., Richardson, J.R., Hill, P.J. & Main, W.deL., 1985: Shallow rock wall biological associations of some southern fiords of New Zealand. *New Zealand Journal of Zoology* 8: 209-227.

Grange, K.R., 1990. Unique marine habitats in the New Zealand fiords: a case for preservation. New Zealand Oceanographic Report 1990/7 prepared for Department of Conservation. 70 pp.

Grange, K.R. & Mladenov, P., 1991. Report on planning workshop – Fiords Marine Research. DSIR Marine & Freshwater and University of Otago.

Grange, K.R. & Goldberg, W., 1992. Diving Doubtful Sound. *Sea Frontiers* 38(4): 44-47.

Grange, K.R. & Goldberg, W., 1993. Fiords down under. *Natural History* 3/93: 60-68

Grimmett, J., 1993. Water-based activities in the Fiordland coastal area. Unpublished Report, Royds Garden Dunedin. 8 inventories.

Habib, G., 1989. Ngai tahu Claim to Mahinga Kai. Waitangi Tribunal, Department of Justice, Wellington.

Hall-Jones, J., 1968. *Early Fiordland*. A.H. & A.W. Reed. 199 pp.

Hall-Jones, J., 1976. *Fiordland Explored*. A.H. & A.W. Reed, Wellington. 148 pp.

Henry, R., 1903. *The Habits of the Flightless Birds of New Zealand*, Wellington.

Hill, S. & Hill, J., 1987. *Richard Henry of Resolution Island*. John McIndoe/NZ Wildlife Service, Dunedin. 364 pp.

Hurley, D.E., 1964: Benthic ecology of Milford Sound. Pp 79-89 in Skerman, T.M. (ed.) Studies of a southern Fiord. *New Zealand Oceanographic Institute Memoir 17*. 101pp.

Kenchington, R.A. & Agardy, M.T., 1990. Achieving marine conservation through biosphere reserve planning and management. *Environmental Conservation* 17: 39-44.

King, J.E. 1983. *Seals of the World*. Oxford University Press. 240 pp.

McCrone, A. (Ed)., 1994. A draft status list for New Zealand's marine flora and fauna. Dept. of Conservation, Wellington. 59pp.

McKnight, D.G. & Estcourt, I.N., 1978. Benthic ecology of Caswell and Nancy Sounds. Pp 85-90 in Glasby, G.P., (ed.), 1978: Fiord studies: Caswell and Nancy Sounds, New Zealand. *New Zealand Oceanographic Memoir 79*. 94 pp.

McShane, P., Mercer, S. & Naylor, R., 1992. Sea-urchins in Dusky Sound – Prospects for a major Kina industry in New Zealand. *New Zealand Professional Fisherman*. December 1992: 34-40.

McShane, P., Stewart, R., Anderson, O. & Gerring, P., 1994. Failure of kina fishery leaves bitter taste. *Seafood New Zealand* 2(4): 33-34.

McShane, P., 1994. Evidence for localised recruitment failure in the New Zealand abalone *Haliotis iris* (Mollusca : Gastropoda). Pp 145-150 in Battershill, C.N. et al., (eds), *Proceedings of the Second International Temperate Reef Symposium*, 7-10 January 1992, Auckland, NZ. NIWA Marine, Wellington. 252 pp.

Meads, M., 1990. *Forgotten Fauna. The rare, endangered, and protected invertebrates of New Zealand*. DSIR Publishing, Wellington. 95 pp.

Nelson, W., and Gordon, D., 1997. *Coastal and Oceanic Biodiversity: A Challenge for New Zealand*. Biodiversity Now Symposium, 1997.

New Zealand Law Commission – pp9, 1989. The Treaty of Waitangi and Maori Fisheries. New Zealand Law Commission Preliminary Paper No. 9. 182 pp.

Olsen G., 1991. Fiordland Marine Reserves – A First? *New Zealand Professional Fisherman* 5(9): 36-38.

Paulin, C.D., 1994. Description of a new genus and two new species of bythitid fishes and a redescription of *Bidenichthys consobrinus* (Hutton) from New Zealand. *Journal of Natural History* 29: 249-258.

Paulin, R., 1889. *The Wild West Coast of New Zealand – A Summer cruise in the "Rosa"*. Thoburn & Company, London. 121 pp.

Peat, N. & Patrick, B., 1996. *Wild Fiordland: Discovering the Natural History of a World Heritage Area*. Dunedin, N.Z. University of Otago Press, 1996. 135 pp.

Pickrill, R.A., 1987. Circulation and sedimentation of suspended particulate matter in New Zealand fjords. *Marine Geology* 74: 21-39.

Powell, P., 1976. *Fishermen of Fiordland*. A.H. & A.W. Reed, Wellington. 119 pp.

Richardson, J.R., 1981. Brachiopods in mud: Resolution of a dilemma. *Science New York* 211(4487): 1161-1163.

Roberts, C.D., 1989. A revision of New Zealand orange perches (Teleostei: Serranidae) previously referred to *Lepidoperca pulchella* (Waite) with description of a new species of *Lepidoperca* from New Zealand. *Journal of Natural History* 23: 557-589.

Southland Regional Council, 1993. Proposed Regional Policy Statement for Southland. *Southland Regional Council Publication* No. 49: 1-214.

Southland Regional Council, 1994. Proposed Regional Coastal Plan, Consultative Draft. Draft 16.10: 1-244.

Waitangi Tribunal-22, 1988. Muriwhenua Fishing Report: Report of the Waitangi Tribunal on the Muriwhenua Fishing Claim. Waitangi Tribunal, Department of Justice, Wellington. 371 pp.

Ward, P.D. 1992. *On Methuselah's Trail: Living Fossils and the Great Extinctions*. W.H. Freeman and Co. New York. 212 pp.

Williams, J.A., 1992. The abundance and distribution of Bottlenose dolphins (*Tursiops truncatus*) in Doubtful Sound. Unpublished M.Sc. Thesis, University of Otago, Dunedin. 58 pp.

Glossary

Adventive – establishment of an organism not usually native to a region.
Algae – seaweed, marine plants which may be single celled (micro-algae) or multicelled and plant-like (macroalgae).
Amphipod – a small laterally compressed crustacean.
Anoxic – without oxygen.
Asexual reproduction – reproduction in which an animal divides into two or more pieces rather than involving eggs and sperm.
Benthic – living on the seafloor.
Biodiversity – the range of different plant and animal species.
Bioluminescence – production of light by living organisms.
Bioprospecting – searching for organisms which may have chemicals of use in the manufacture of medicines or industry.
Bivalve – a mollusc with two hinged shells, e.g. scallop.
Byssal threads – a tuft of strong filaments used by bivalves to anchor the shell to the seafloor.
Calcareous – composed of lime (calcium carbonate), the hard material of shells and coral skeletons.
Cephalopod – a mollusc with tentacles e.g., octopus, squids.
Cilia – short hair-like structures protruding from cells which beat rhythmically to induce a current of water for feeding or locomotion.
Coelenterate – a radially symmetrical invertebrate, e.g. coral, sea anemone.
Crustacean – an invertebrate animal with a hard exterior skeleton and jointed limbs, e.g. crab, crayfish.
Detritus – fine material formed from decomposing organisms.
Diatoms – single celled planktonic algae.
Echinoderm – a marine animal with a five sided symmetry, e.g., starfish, sea-urchin.
Ecology – study of organisms and their environment.
Endemic – native and restricted to a certain region.
Epiphyte – a plant which uses another as a support for growth (not parasitic).
Fauna – all animals found in an area.
Filter, feeder – an organism which feeds by straining food particles from the water.
Flora – all plants found in an area.
Frond – leaf of a seaweed.
Gastropod – a mollusc with a single shell (univalve), e.g. limpet, whelk.
Genus – a classification used to group related species.
Hermaphrodite – an organism possessing both male and female organs.
Holdfast – root-like base used by algae to attach to the seafloor.
Holothurian – echinoderm with a sausage shaped body and the skeleton reduced to small spicules, e.g., sea-cucumber.
Ichthyofauna – fish fauna.
Invertebrate – animals which lack a backbone.
Isopod – a small flattened crustacean.
Larvae – immature life stage.
Lophophore – a ciliated tentacle used for food gathering.
Molluscs – a group of invertebrate animals with soft bodies and a muscular foot, often encased in a hard shell, e.g., bivalves, gastropods, cephalopods.
Operculum – lid or cover, e.g. gill cover of a fish or 'cat's-eye' of gastropod.
Parasitic – a relationship between two organisms in which is of benefit to one at the expense of the other.
Papillae – small conical projection of skin.
Pathogen – disease causing micro-organism.
Pelagic – free-swimming.
Photosynthesis – process by which plants manufacture carbohydrates from carbon dioxide and water in the presence of light and chlorophyll.
Phylum – a group of related organisms, e.g., all Molluscs.
Plankton – organisms which drift or swim weakly in the ocean, includes plants (phytoplankton) and animals (zooplankton). Also microorganisms or organic particles (picoplankton).
Polychaete – a segmented marine worm with bristles.
Proboscis – anterior trunk-like process.
Sessile – fixed in place.
Species – a single lineage of organisms defined by distinct characters.
Stolon – a cylindrical stem-like structure.
Symbiotic – a partnership between two unrelated organsms which is of benefit to both.
Zooid – individual animal within a colonial organism.
Zooxanthid – colonial coelenterate resembling a cluster of sea anemones.

Index

A

Acanthoclinus 130, 131
Acanthoclinus matti 131
Acanthogorgia breviflora 44
Adeonellopsis sp. 115
Aegogropila sp. 38
Alces alces 152
Alcyonium aurantiacum 59
algae 18, 26, 28, 29, 32, 36, 41, 50, 74, 76, 81, 82, 86, 88, 92, 105, 106, 116, 128, 129, 131, 166
Allostichaster insignus 99
Amaurochiton glaucus 79
amphipod 89, 108
Amphithyris richardsonae 72
Annelida 60
Anthothoe albocincta 54
Antipathes fiordensis 44, 46, 49
Archidoris wellingtonensis 77, 81
Arctocephalus forsteri 142
Argobuccium tumidum 79
ascidians 116, 118, 119, 120
Asterodon miliaris 99, 104
Astraea heliotropium 79, 80, 89
Astrobrachion constrictum 47, 100, 102
Astroceras elegans 102
Astronomer Point 124
Astrostole scabra 98, 99
Atrina zelandica 76, 78
Aulacomya atra 76, 78
Austrosimulium spp. 159, 160, 162
Axinella tricalyciformis 38, 42, 43

B

ballast water 20, 174
banded perch 131, 140
banded wrasse 128
barnacles 16, 28, 76, 84, 92
batwinged cannibal fly 160
bioactive compounds 41, 166
Biosphere Reserve 183, 185
biscuit star 99
Bitectipora sp. 115
bivalves 74
black coral 12, 13, 19, 23, 28, 36, 38, 44, 47, 48, 49, 50, 86, 96, 101, 102, 108, 116, 120, 166
Blanket Bay 128
blue cod 105, 127, 128, 132, 170, 172
blue dot triplefin 131
blue eye triplefin 131
blue penguin 145, 147, 151
blue-lipped mussel 76
Botrylloides sp 116, 122
bottlenose dolphin 19, 20, 145, 147, 148
brachiopods 12, 19, 68, 70, 71, 72, 73, 164, 166
brackish water mussel 76
brackish water snail 79
Breaksea Sound 115, 158
bristleworm 64
brittlestar 94, 97, 99, 101
brotula 132, 133, 167
Bryozoans 102, 112, 114, 115, 116, 166, 177
bull kelps 30
butterfish 128
butterfly chitons 79
butterfly perch 10, 13, 124, 126, 128

C

Caesioperca lepidoptera 47, 124, 128
Calcarea 36, 38
Callanthias allporti 127, 131
Calliostoma granti 79, 80
Calliostoma tigris 79, 80
Callyspongia latituba 38, 42
Callyspongia ramosa 38
Cancer novaezelandiae 89, 92
Carpomitra costata 34
Capra hircus 152
Carex pleiostachys 152
carpet shark 131, 134
Carpophyllum sp 26, 28, 32
Caryophyllia profunda 44, 49
Caswell Sound 28, 102
cats 154, 157
cat's eye 74, 79
Caulerpa 28, 30
Cellaria pilosa 115
Cellaria tenuirostris 115
Cerianthus sp 44
Cerianthus bollonsi 54
Cervus elephas 152
cetaceans 145, 166
Champia sp 28, 30
Charonia lampas 79, 82
circular saw shell 79, 80, 89
CITES 49
Clathrina coreacea 38
clingfishes 131
Cnemidocarpa bicornuta 119
cockle 79
Codium fragile 28
coelenterates 44
Comanthus benhami 164
commercial fishing 13, 145, 166, 170, 174, 180, 181, 184
common roughy 131
common triplefin 131

INDEX 189

conger eel 131
Conger verreauxi 131
Cook 140, 152, 154, 164
Cookia sulcata 79, 80, 81
Cook's scurvy grass 152
coralline algae 28, 36, 41
Corals 6, 12, 18, 19, 44, 47, 48, 49, 57, 59, 112, 172, 177
Corhiza ritchiei 50
Coscinasterias calamaria 76, 94, 96
crabs 84, 86, 88, 89, 92, 108
Crania huttoni 72
crayfish 22, 23, 76, 81, 84, 86, 87, 102, 105, 170, 172, 174, 177
Crepidacantha sp. 115
Cribricellina cribraria 115
Crinoidea 94
cruise vessels 174
crustaceans 6, 47, 64, 84, 166
cryptic fish 128
Cryptoconchus porosus 78
Culicea rubeola 57, 59
cushion star 82
Cyclopecten transenna ?
Cystophora sp. 28, 30
Cystophora platylobium 30

D

Dacrycarpus dacrydioides 152
Dacrydium cupressinum 152
Deep Cove 115, 166, 174, 180
deep water emergence 164
Dellichthys morelandi 131
demosponges 36, 38
Department of Conservation 6, 7, 24, 142, 154, 157, 166, 170, 178, 181, 185
Desmophyllum cristagalli 44, 49
diatoms 26, 164
Didemnum candidum 116, 119
Diloma zelandica 79
divers 44, 49, 50, 86, 112, 127, 128, 131, 132, 138, 145, 164, 174, 177, 180, 181
Doubtful Sound 13, 19, 20, 38, 50, 72, 102, 105, 115, 128, 131, 147, 166, 172, 174, 180
Durvillaea antarctica 30
Durvillaea spp. 26
Durvillaea willana 30
Dusky Sound 105, 152, 162, 164, 170, 182

E

Echinocardium cordatum 106
Echinoderms 6, 64, 94, 101, 108, 164
Echinoidea 94
Echiura 60
Ecklonia sp. 28, 30, 32, 34, 105

Edwardsia sp. 52
electrophoresis 49
elephant seals 145
Elminius modestus 76, 84
Enteromorpha 28
Eptatretus cirrhatus 131
Epymenia sp. ?
Errina novaezelandiae 44, 49, 92
Escharoides sp. 115
estuarine triplefin 131
Eubalaena australis 145
Eudyptes minor 147
Eudyptes pachyrhynchus 147
Euryolambus australis 89
Eurystomella 115
Evechinus chloroticus 76, 102
Exochella 115
Exul singularis 160

F

fan shell 79, 81
featherstars 12, 94, 97, 106, 108, 164
Felis catus 154
Fenestrulina 115
ferns 152
ferrets 154, 158
Figularia sp 115
filter feeders 74
Fiordichthys slartibartfasti 132, 133
Fiordland crested penguin 147, 148, 149, 150, 151
Fiordland skink 158, 159
fisheries 7, 22, 24, 129, 135, 170, 174, 178, 181, 183
Fissidentalium zelandicum 81
flatworms 60, 63
flower urchin 94
Forsterygion flavonigrum 133, 138
Forsterygion lapillum 131
Forsterygion malcolmi 131, 133
Foveolaria sp 115
freshwater layer 13, 16, 26, 28, 30, 47, 50, 52, 76, 84, 86, 94, 96, 98, 101, 106
fur seals 142, 145

G

Gaidropsarus novaezelandiae 131
Galaxias argenteus 124
Galaxias fasciatus 124
galaxiid 124
gastropod 74, 79, 99, 106, 108
George Forster 124, 154, 164
giant kokopu 124
girdled wrasse 128
glass sponges 36
goats 152

Gobiesocidae 131
gorgonians 44, 98, 102
Gracilaria secundata ??
Grahamina nigripenne 131
Grant's maurea 79
green chiton 79
green false oyster 79
Gregarinidra sp 115
grooved fan shell 79
groper 132, 135, 172
Guardians of Fiordland's fisheries 22, 24

H

Hadramphus stilbocarpae 158
Hagfish 131, 138
Halecium beanii 50
Haliotis iris 79
Hall's totara 152
Harrison Cove 174, 177
heart urchins 94, 106
Helicolenus percoides 128, 136
Hemerocoetes spp 131
Henricia lukinsii 99
Henry, Richard 150, 157, 158
hermit crabs 84, 88, 89, 92
Hirudinea 64
Holothuroidea 94
Hooker's sealions 145
horse mussel 76, 78, 177
hydrocorals 12, 18, 49
Hydrodendron sp 50
hydroids 6, 44, 50, 80, 81, 119
Hydrurga leptonyx 145
Hymenena sp 28
Hypoplectrodes huntii 131
Hypsistozoa fasmaria 60

I

isopod 89, 108

J

jack mackerel 132, 145
Jacquinotia edwardsi 89
James Cook 124, 142, 152, 170
Jason mirabilis 77
Jasus edwardsii 76, 84, 87
Jasus verreauxi 86
jock stewart 128, 136

K

kahikatea 152
kakapo 154, 157, 158, 159, 162
kamahi 152
kea 161

kina 166
knobbled weevils 158
Kophobolemnon sp. 48

L

lace corals 112
lamp shell 68
Latridopsis ciliaris 127
Latrunculia brevis 38
leatherjackets 41
leeches 64
Leiolopisma acrinasum 158, 159
leopard seal 145
Lepidium oleraceum 152
Lepidoperca tasmanica 126, 127
Leptoclinides sp. 116
Leptomithrax sp 86, 92
Leucettusa lancifer 38
limpets 74
Liothyrella neozelandea 72
Litoria ewingi 154
liverworts 152
Livoneca raynaudii 89
lophophore 68, 70
Lotella rhacinus 131
Lucinoma galatheae 81
lugworms 64

M

Macrocystis 10, 28, 30, 84
Macrocystis pyrifera 28, 29, 30
Magasella sanguinea 71, 72
Maoricolpus roseus 76, 80, 99
Margaretta barbata 115
Marginariella sp. 30, 34
Marginariella boryana 28
marine reserves 22, 24, 174, 180, 181
Megadyptes antipodes 150
Mendosoma lineatum 124, 131
Mesopeplum convexum 79
Metrosideros umbellata 152
Microporella 115
Milford Underwater Observatory 7, 50, 174, 176, 177
Milford, Milford Sound 7, 13, 14, 16, 20, 23, 28, 30, 115, 124, 145, 147, 152, 160, 172, 174, 177, 180, 181, 182
Mimteridium cryptum 52
Ministry of Fisheries 172, 174, 178, 181
Mirounga leonina 145, 146
moki 124, 127
molluscs 6, 16, 68, 71, 73, 74, 76, 81, 82, 88, 89, 92, 99,106, 108, 164, 166
Monomyces flabellum 57
moose 152
moss animals 112

mosses 152
mottled sandstar 101
mottled triplefin 131, 133
Mucropetraliella sp 115
Museum of New Zealand 6, 10, 18, 76, 101, 124, 127, 132, 166, 168
mussel, mussels 16, 28, 50, 74, 76, 78, 86, 94, 96, 98, 103, 177
Mustela erminea 154
Mustela furo 154
Mustela nivalis 154
Mycale sp. 38
Mytilus galloprovincialis 76, 78
myzostomes 64

N

Nancy Sound 131
National Parks 7, 14, 178, 180
Neilo australis 81
Nemadactylus macropterus 127
Nematoda 60
Nematodes 63
Nemertinea 60
Neothyris lenticularis 68
Nestor notabilis 61
neptune's necklace 28
New Zealand Oceanographic Institute 164
Ngai tahu 170, 174
NIWA 6, 36, 49, 79, 81, 86, 112, 128, 166, 168
Nothofagus menziesii 152, 154
Notoclinops caerulepunctus 130, 131
Notoclinops segmentatus 131, 133
Notoclinus fenestratus 124
Notolabrus celidotus 128
Notolabrus cinctus 128
Notolabrus fucicola 128, 129
Notomithrax sp. 92
Notornis mantelli 156, 157
Notosaria nigricans 71, 72
Nudibranchs 41, 74, 77, 81

O

Obelia australis 50
oblique swimming triplefins 131, 133, 134
Obliquichthys maryannae 133, 134
Ocnus brevidentis 106, 110
octopuses 74, 81, 82, 145
Octopus huttoni 81, 82
Octopus maorum 81
Odax pullus 128
Opaeophora sp 115
opalfish 131
Ophionereis fasciata 101
Orthoscuticella 115
Otago Museum 160
Otionella 115

Oxycomanthus plectrophorum 97, 108

P

Palaemon affinis 84
Paphies australis 79
Parapercis colias 127, 128, 129, 132
Parapercis gilliesi 128
Paratrachichthys trailli 131
Patiriella regularis 76, 96, 103
peanutworms 60, 63, 64
Paua 82, 166, 170, 172
Paulin, Robert 10, 12, 24, 49, 132, 142, 154, 162, 185
Pecten novaezelandiae 76, 82
Pectinura maculata 97, 101, 109
pelagic tunicates 118, 122
Pentagonaster pulchellus 99, 107
Phocarctos hookeri 145
Physeter catodon 145, 146
phytoplankton 16, 26
Pickersgill Harbour 124
pigs 152
Pilayella sp. 28
Pilayella littoralis 28
Pinnoctopus cordiformis 81
pipi 79
plankton 12, 18, 49, 102, 105, 131, 166
Platyhelminthes 60
Podocarpus cunninghamii 152
polychaeta 64
polychaetes 64, 108
Polymastia croceus 42
Polyprion oxygeneios 132
Pomatoceros caeruleus 64
possum 20, 152
Potamopyrgus estuarinus 79
Pratulum pulchellum 81
prawns 89
Preservation Inlet 14, 72, 102, 106, 145, 164, 170, 184
Protula bispiralis 62, 64
Pseudechinus sp. 47, 102, 105
Pseudechinus albocincta 106
Pseudechinus huttoni. 16
Pseudolabrus miles 128
Psuedophycis bachus 127
pycnogonids 84, 88
Pyrosoma atlanticum 118

R

Ralfsia sp. 28
rata 152
rats 154, 157, 158, 160
Rattus norvegicus 154
Rattus rattus 154
recreational fishery 86

recreational fishing 20, 172, 174, 181
red cod 127
red coral 44, 49, 92, 172
red deer 152
Resolution Island 158
Resource Management Act 178
Reterebellid polychaetes 64
Rhabdozoum wilsoni 115
Rhodymenia sp 28, 76
ribbed mussel 76, 78
ribbonworms 60
right whales 145
rimu 30, 152
rock cod 131
rock lobster 23, 86, 87, 135, 166, 170, 172, 173
rock lobster fishery 86, 172
rockfishes 130, 131
rockling ?
roundworms 60
Ruditapes largillierti 76

S

Sabellid polychaetes 64
Saccoglossus sp. 62
Salacia buski 50
salps 96, 118, 122, 132
sandfly 7, 160
Sarcophyllum bollonsi 164
Sargassum sinclairii 26
scallops 74, 76, 82, 166, 172
scarlet wrasse 128
Sclerasterias mollis 96
Sclerasterias mollis 64
Sclerosponges 36
Scorpaena papillosus 124, 131
scorpionfish 124, 131
Scrupocellaria 115
scuba divers 44, 49, 86, 164
Scutus breviculus 79, 82
sea anemones 57, 77
sea lettuce 16, 26, 28, 76
sea pens 13, 44, 46, 48, 164
sea spiders 84, 88
sea-cucumber 94, 96, 106, 108, 110
sea-horses 129
sea-lilies 94, 108
sea-slugs 77, 81
sea-squirts 18, 119
sea-urchins 12, 16, 28, 30, 47, 82, 94, 102, 106, 110, 131
seaperch 128, 136
seaweed 26, 49, 16, 20, 26, 30, 86, 166
segmented worms 60, 64
Serpulid polychaetes 64
Sertularella geodiae 51
Sertularella robusta 50
Sertularia marginata 50

seven-armed starfish 99
shield shell 74, 79, 82
shrimp 84, 88, 89, 104, 108
silver beech 152, 154
Sipuncula 60
Smittina sp. 115
Smittoidea sp. 115
snakestars 47, 51, 96, 97, 99, 100, 101, 109, 166
snapper 105
soft coral 44
Solegnathus spinossissimus 128, 140
solitary corals 44, 49
Southland Regional Council 178
spider crab 86, 89
spiny dogfish 127, 131
spiny seadragons 128
splendid perch 13, 127, 129, 131, 167
splendid rockfish 131
sponges 6, 12, 13, 36, 38, 39, 41, 42, 47, 59, 62, 64, 77, 86, 92, 102, 115, 116, 118, 119, 126, 136, 166
spotties 128
Squalus acanthias 127, 131
squid 74, 145, 150
starfish 64, 76, 82, 94, 96, 98, 99, 103, 104, 107, 109
Steginoporella sp 115
Stelleroidea 94
Stenogramme interrupta 28
Stichopus mollis 106, 110
Stictosiphonia vaga 28
Stilbocarpa lyalli 158
stoats 150, 154, 157, 158
Strawberry Fields 106, 185
strawberry sea-cucumber 106
Strigops habroptilus 154, 157
Sus scrofa 152
Symplectella rowei 38
Symplectoscyphus subarticulatus 48, 50

T

takahe 157, 158
Talochlamys gemmulata 79, 81, 82
tarakihi 127
Te Wahipounamu 13, 24, 152, 178, 183, 185
telescope fish 124, 131, 138
Thallaseleotris 131
The Gut 44, 131, 174
Thorecta new species 42
tiger shell 79, 80
topshell 79, 81
tourism 23, 170, 174, 183
Toxopneustes pileolus 94
Trachurus spp 132
tree-slip 23
triangle crabs 89
Tricellaria sp. 115

Trichosurus vulpecula 152
triplefins 13, 16, 130, 131, 133, 134, 138, 140
Trochus viridis 81
trumpet shell 79, 82
tube anemone 12, 54, 177
tube worm 65, 99, 177
turban shell 79, 80, 81
Turbo smaragdus 79
turret shell 76, 79, 80
Tursiops truncatus 19, 145, 148
tusk shells 81

U

Ulva lactuca 28
Ulva spp. 76
UNESCO World Heritage Committee, World Heritage list 13, 24, 174, 178, 183, 185
University of Canterbury 150, 166
University of Otago 49, 115, 166
urchin clingfish 131
urchins 26, 76, 106, 131

V

Valdemunitella sp 115
Venerupis largillierti 99
virgin paua 79
Voluntary Code of Practice 180

W

Wairaki Island 158
Waltonia inconspicua ?
wavy line perch 126, 127
weasels 154, 158
weedfish 124
Weinmannia racemosa 152
whales 145, 146
whaling 145, 170
whistling frog 154
white sea-urchin 16, 47, 110
Wittrockiella lyallii 26

X

Xenostrobus securis 76

Y

yellow weevers 128
yellow-black triplefin 131, 133, 138
yellow-eyed penguin 150

Z

Zeacumantus subcarinatus 79
Zonaria turneriana 34

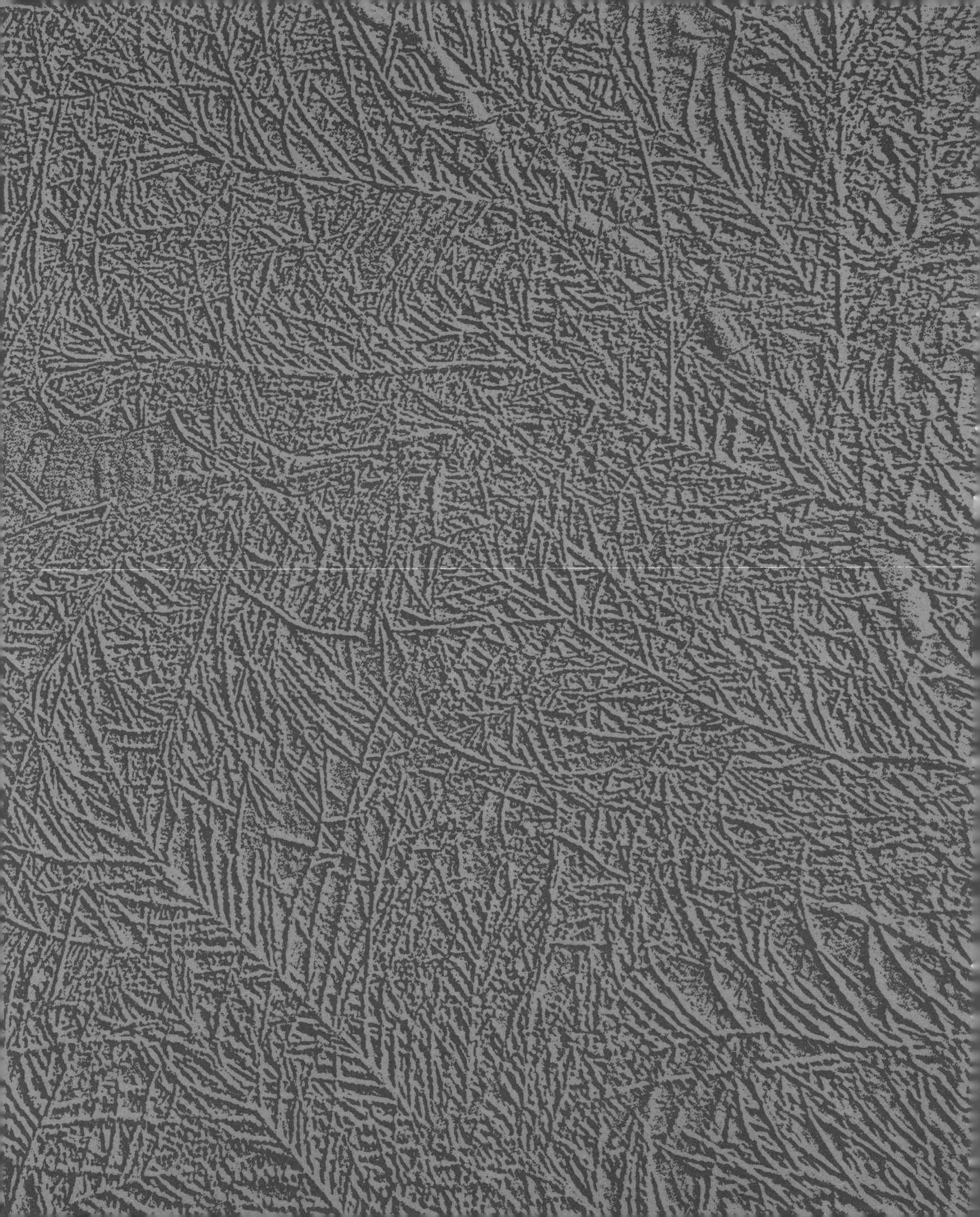